This Family Business

THE FAMILY AT WORK

Mark Lee

CHRISTIAN PUBLICATIONS

Camp Hill, Pennsylvania

The mark of vibrant faith

The following publishers have generously given permission to use quotations from copyrighted works:
From *Who Am I and What Am I Doing Here?*, by Mark
Lee. Copyright 1980 by Mott Media, Inc. From *The Art
of Japanese Management*, by Richard Tanner Pascale
and Anthony G. Athos. Reprinted by permission of
Simon & Schuster, A Division of Gulf & Western Corporation. From "Oedipus in the Board Room," by Daniel
Goleman. Reprinted from PSYCHOLOGY TODAY
MAGAZINE, copyright 1977, Ziff-Davis Company and
used by permission. Permission from Simon & Schuster
was also granted for quotes from *The Name Game*, by
Christopher Anderson and *Families*, by Jane Howard.

Library of Congress Catalog Card Number: 82-73873
ISBN: 0-87509-328-0

To those families I have known who have modeled Christian life: parents and children with integrity for ethical living, with energy and creativity for service. They were devotional in their spirits, generous in their acts, exciting in their relationships, and forward looking in their perceptions for problem solving. This book is ascribed to them.

Contents

Preface

By the time of the American bicentennial year, 1976, a family in the United States required greater resources and more of just about everything than a small family business required a century earlier. Some village businesses in 1876 grossed no more than one or two hundred thousand dollars in the generation of their founders and owners. Even of those businesses that were considered to do well, many netted no more than a half million dollars. According to a 1977 study, a middle-class family manages three quarters of a million dollars in personal income from marriage initiation until the death of the breadwinner. Analysts in 1980 projected that many families would take in a million or more dollars in one generation with little to show for it at the conclusion.

A small business during the nineteenth century paid few, if any, direct taxes. The owner or manager maintained simple books and accounts. Most transactions were cash exchange. His purchases outside of bulk merchandise were few. He owned no expensive machinery or equipment.

The modern family must keep track of extensive income and expenditures, maintain records, keep insurance and bank accounts, and pay community, state and federal taxes that would have boggled the mind of a cracker-barrel store owner. Some families use small home computers to keep their affairs in order. Equipment in the modern, bicentennial home exceeds even the grandest fantasies of kings or businessmen in the centennial year of the United States. During the twentieth century, electrically powered equipment became a reality. Now more work is accomplished in minutes than hand utensils and tools wielded for hours could accomplish in former times.

The comparison of the modern family to the nineteenth-century home is even more dramatic than the comparison to a business. A centennial farmer in 1876 could sustain his family on the western plains with a team of horses, a few simple tools, wagon, plow, harness, and a quarter section of land. Perhaps a sod house or cabin would be deemed adequate for a bride who initiated homemaking with an open fireplace, an iron stove, and rough-hewn furniture. Three, four or five hundred dollars got the family underway on American and Canadian frontiers. Farmland cost nothing for the American western homesteader. The Homestead Act signed by President Abraham Lincoln during the early 1860s gave thousands of square miles of land in small plots (generally 180 acres) to any citizens who would farm the land. Hard work was about all that was required of the frontier family, and hard work was about all there was to do. Church and community festivals provided some diversion. Easterners, at the time of the American centennial, enjoyed greater refinement and more domestic accoutrements in their homes, but even that was impressive only in comparison to harsh western life.

Before urbanization a family fairly well ran itself, with family members sharing labors. The environment offered some recreation for adults and children in the settings of home, nature or work. Environmental limits and slow transportation controlled the quality of life. With the rise of the big city, work moved from direct family labor, such as farming, to labor for a wage or salary. This urbanization, coupled with the growing desire of ordinary citizens to acquire material goods, changed life from the naturalness of a controlled rural environment guided by nature and family needs to the complex life of the city. Such changes required a new creativity in order to succeed.

In an urbanized society, cycles of economic boom and bust threatened the life of the nation. As late as 1939-40, at the close of the Great Depression, many urban families survived on weekly incomes of fifteen dollars. In 1935 the standard wage in some depressed areas for a farm worker was a dollar a day. Throughout the decades that preceded the national depression, millions of families knew poverty as standard fare. The few moguls who lived in luxury and gained publicity for wealth did not reflect reality for the masses. In the following decades, the rich began to influence the expectations of the common man, and the middle class became massive and affluent, dominating national life.

Ultimately, the electronics communications media ended rural isolation. The whole population became homogenized with what might be called "urban" or "mass perceptions." Mechanization and mobility ended the way of life created by the isolated family farm and small town. Today a family must be concerned with management of life savings, spending, planning, education, investments, insurance, health benefits, personal taxes, licenses, laws, houses, recreation, travel, media, urbanization, environment, and modern institutions. A new complexity has entered common life.

One of the crucial factors in this modern, urban complexity is that a family, like a business, needs excellent management. Yet most families do not develop skills necessary to manage large material acquisitions and urban relationships for the best good of themselves and the society. Perhaps this century is a learning period, so that mistakes are to be expected and endured. Things may improve when we learn to manage ourselves in our concreted, electrified cities. And there are analysts who argue that we could return to simplicity in living if we would reduce our consumerism attitudes and values. Expectations seem to be falling a bit.

We can do better, much better than we believe we can.

The purpose of this book is to urge parents to learn about management of family life in the late twentieth-century environment, even if it remains complex, and to put what they learn into effect for the benefit of both family and society. This work is based on a Christian point of view. It is assumed that the Christian family is generally perceived as an ideal, but possible in the current society. It was effective in the rural society. It can be in the urban.

In the five sections that follow there is no priority represented in the order except for the first: Personnel. All considerations here start with persons, those serving and being served. We need to know who they are, why they do the things they do, and how their perceptions of identity affect them and others. In section two contracts are introduced as effective means for guiding conduct and solving family problems. Some contracts are legal, binding before a court of law, but require covenants and agreements based on love and good will to meet or forestall differences between family members. The third section reviews the matter of goals and objectives. Adopting this way of life, a family may determine by its objectives what it wishes to do and how it can determine its own success. In section four, family organization is focused through administration, work, and funding. The family becomes a small business enterprise, humane and manageable. Finally, in section five, the important matters of philosophy, principally faith, ethics and social understanding complete this focus on the family and its dynamic model as an institution.

This volume does not include extensive materials that appear in other books or articles I have written on family themes. Some short outlines on specific points are repeated here for clarity. References to selected earlier writings of mine are made in the recommended readings at the end of chapters in the belief that more complete understanding of my views will be gained if those as well as other supporting materials are investigated. Several secular titles are cited.

It is customary, at the outset of a work, to acknowledge persons who have contributed significantly to the production of a writer. For several years two persons have devoted primary interest, time and skills to my writing projects. One is my wife, Fern, who reviews my work and provides insights that inspire me to make important editings. The other is my secretary, Yvonne Cederblom, whose typing skills, knowledge of our language, and patience have certainly increased my productivity beyond any goal I had set for myself in early years. I am grateful, too, for the support of the Simpson College trustees, who have, without reservation, permitted me to follow lines of professional interests and activities I feel are my own. Certainly a skillful editor helps one say better what an author wishes to say. Diane Zimmerman has served admirably in that role.

Section One
PERSONNEL

CHAPTER 1 • *Persons*
Persons serving and being served in appropriate ways
become a major consideration in business planning, in
Christian ministry, and in family unity.

CHAPTER 2 • *Motivation*
Whether for business, ministry, or family purposes, people
tend to do what they are stimulated to do, and those actions for which they feel they will be rewarded.

CHAPTER 3 • *Identity*
Every individual or institution seeks recognition, and that
recognition is found, in part, through the name and home
of the business, the ministry, or the family.

CHAPTER 1

Persons

- Who are the personnel and customers for a business?

- Who are the members of a family?

This should be your ambition: to live a quiet life, minding your own business and doing your work, just as we told you before. As a result, people who are not Christians will trust and respect you, and you will not need to depend on others for enough money to pay your bills (1 Thess. 4:11-12, TLB).

Businesses categorize persons according to their functions related to those businesses. From the general population appear the customers, the servers, the suppliers, the managers and the investors. Relationships between these personnel groups in business have their counterparts in family life.

Business Concepts in the New Testament

The word *business* appears several times in the New Testament. It commonly refers to personal, family or church affairs. The biblical text above illustrates the point. The Apostle Paul recommends that the Thessalonians be ambitious to achieve the various personal accomplishments he lists. One of these is to live a tranquil or peaceful life. To so live, an individual or family must give adequate attention to those personal affairs making up their main day-to-day business. Fulfillment is achieved, the apostle states, by taking responsibility for oneself. If able, each person should do his own work. He does not presume that another should do it. Even so, we know from other texts that family members ought to take responsibility for relatives in need. There are always those who, regardless of how self-sufficient they might wish to be, will need assistance.

One result obtained when this pattern of self and family responsibility is followed is respect from friends and neighbors. Respect stimulates trust, and trust generally motivates persons to act favorably toward those they respect. Paul informs the Thessalonians that non-Christians observing the responsible behavior of believers will develop affirmative attitudes toward Christians, a preliminary to their own discovery of faith. The consistent Christian, thus, does his duty in both personal and family affairs, and his successful family performance inspires respect and trust for that family and its beliefs.

In addition to an affirmative reputation among unbelievers, a second result is implied in private personal satisfaction. The "successful" Christian has been self-reliant—others have not had to pay his bills or carry other obligations he is competent to bear.

The word *business* also appears in the Epistle to the Romans. The Apostle Paul utilized the Greek word *spoude* when he wrote: *Be not slothful in business* (12:11). His emphasis is on one's occupation: "Do not be lazy in your work." Work is to be done, the Greek word implies, with dispatch, eagerness, earnestness and diligence. In the idiom there is an element of appropriate speed, but not hastiness. It carries the meaning that one should eagerly do his duty.

In the last chapter of Romans (16:2) the word *pragma* appears. Our English word *pragmatic* derives from *pragma*, and is used to mean "practical" or "applied" or "workable." The apostle opened the concluding chapter of Romans with commendation of Phoebe: *She has worked hard in the church* (TLB). Phoebe's diligence in Christian labor was attractive to Paul.

The practicality of the term *business* in the Bible is further illustrated in another term used in Acts 6:3. Here

Luke records the instructions from the apostles to the young church to select deacons who are spiritual men, wise and with excellent reputations. The apostles announce, *We will put them in charge of this business* (TLB). The business of deacons in this instance was to oversee the social program of the church; namely, the distribution of goods to needy Christian families, perhaps also to those who had deposited their wealth in the common treasury. The point here is that administrative positions were given to persons of spiritual integrity who might be expected to be responsible, Spirit-filled and wise, as well as respected by the people. They would do their work well and win support for church programs. The competent manner in which church business is administered presumably inspires confidence in all who observe, and that confidence is helpful for ministry.

When relevant Scriptures such as these on management themes are brought together, an important generalization emerges. It is that scriptural management principles apply along the whole of life. Wherever Christians are instructed about the business of their lives, those learnings hold for all individuals in all situations. They may be functioning in different roles as ministers, or businessmen, or family members. But they are not fragmented or divided as whole persons. The implication of this personal Christian principle is that my "business" should be to care for myself and meet the needs of others who, for some reason, cannot care for themselves. By meeting these needs, I show Christian concern for my family and my neighbors. First concern or duty for each of us should be for those of our own household (1 Tim. 5:8). I am a member of the household so I have a duty to myself. This makes sense because opportunity inherits in proximity and becomes obvious. Opportunity is available. Wider service follows from effective beginnings with those most intimately identified with us. Any genuineness and virtue in the larger service is partly dependent on humble performance of the nearer service. There is efficient stewardship in this pattern—

serving those nearest to us for their good.

Business Relates to Persons

Ideally, business serves persons well. This service to individuals ought to be its large ultimate purpose. It can be perceived and engaged in even when the worker feels his duties are remote from consumers. A machinist, an automobile assembly line worker, a salesman, a pilot, or any other worker or craftsman should be conscious of service orientation, especially his own. He should be reminded from time to time that persons actually use the product he fabricates, or service he performs. Therefore he should make it or do it well. This understanding ought to extend to everyone in any business. A manager, far removed from ten thousand employees under him, should be profoundly aware of them, and the people affected by them. If he is, his conduct of management ought to be affected for their good.

Customers are persons needing or wanting something that a business provides. A flourishing company matches that need or desire with the product or service to the satisfaction of the customer and profit for the business.

For that business to succeed in meeting customer needs, efficient management must be at work. Tolerances are narrow for success or failure. Businesses useful to the welfare of a community often fail or operate at less than optimum levels because management is inefficient. Inefficiency is sometimes nothing more than neglect or laziness—attitudes of unconcern for others. Authorities in business fields know that the key to a corporation's success is generally found in the effectiveness of its management. New management, stepping into the place of old, can turn failure into success, relying on the same product, the same personnel, the same customers. And, new amateur management can destroy, in short order, a firm that has been successful and well nurtured for decades.

There are several management patterns available for running businesses successfully, if success is defined pri-

marily as earning profits. But not all these patterns are
attractive or useful to the purpose of this book. Some
business practices are so objectionable to perceptive citizens that they reject, or nearly so, any analogy that applies
business life to family life. Just as we who appreciate the
family will not reject it because many families fail and
break up, so we will not diminish business because some
philosophies and practices of businessmen are unethical,
self-dealing, and misdirected.

So strongly does the Levinson Institute of Cambridge,
Massachusetts, hold to the concept of family perceptions
for analysis of business or corporation problems that the
consultants of the Institute become "therapists" to their
clients. Founded by Harry Levinson, a clinical psychologist, (his ideas springing from student days, with the
eminent Menningers and David Rapaport) the Institute
has, for more than a quarter of a century, provided what
might be termed *corporate family therapy* to businesses.
Eminent companies like IBM, and government entities like
the Department of State, have utilized the services of the
Institute (Goleman 1977, 45). Perhaps the most significant
objection to the Levinson approach is that it takes the
Freudian model as base for analysis. Freudian theory has
come under heavy critical fire during recent years.

Levinson believes that corporations share many characteristics of the family. Writing about Levinson, Daniel
Goleman states:

'All organizations,' Levinson says, 'recapitulate the basic
family structure in a culture. Our earliest experiences
with our parents are repeated in our subsequent relationships with authority. . . . If everyone knows what the
rules are, things run smoothly. . . . A business and a family share similar psychodynamics' (Goleman 1977, 45).

Drawing from the family, Levinson perceives distinctive
"personalities" with "style and outlook" in large corpo-

rations. As in the family, the abuse of power threatens har-
mony in a corporation, and may destroy the company. In
family-owned businesses Levinson may find "a reenact-
ment of the rivalry between son and father for the mother"
(Goleman 1977, 45). Levinson points out that there are, or
were, maternalistic companies like AT&T, affectionately
called "Ma Bell," and carrying personality appeal. Workers
seeking the benefits of Ma Bell's *family* found the corporation congenial. IBM, says Levinson, was paternalistic
during the regime of Thomas Watson, the founder. Sears,
Roebuck became more egalitarian than IBM. Each company
could identify its happiest employees as those compatible
with the company personality:

> As most people find their own families more congenial
> than others, so they are more at home with a certain
> kind of corporate personality (Goleman 1977, 46).

Levinson found that Italian families, giving the father a
strong place in the home, provide excellent second-in-
command foremen working for a paternalistic boss.
Germans do well in industry where precision and quality
control are important—the consequence of discipline. He
found that the FBI in the United States attracted many
Irish-Catholics because of the rigid structure, something
learned in the parochial schools many of them attended.
According to Levinson, the exceptional executive acts
like a good parent. The four things, he concluded, marking
the fine parent are: (1) a desire that the child should be independent, (2) a desire that the child will be flexible and
roll with the punches, (3) a desire that the child will be
happier than the parent, and (4) a desire that the child po-
sesses high moral standards. Levinson believes these apply
in business bosses as well as in parents—at least they
should apply (Goleman 1977, 46).
Just as stress in a family is absorbed by parents or
passed out to other members of the family, so is stress
kept, or "unloaded downward," by executives. All this

causes pain, and pain calls for a doctor (therapist). The therapist (consultant) may be Levinson:

> The real problems are always deeper than the ones I'm called in for. In all such problems, it's very much like what happens in a family when a kid is in trouble: there is massive denial that anything's wrong until the problem erupts. . . .
>
> An acquisition and merger is like a divorce and remarriage. The executive who stays with the new owners is like the parent who gets custody of the kids. The employees of the acquired company are like foster children. . . .
>
> I often hear people in an acquired company say, "It was just like a family here, but now it's just a big company" (Goleman 1977, 51).

Several excellent businesses inspire the analogy to the family. Following World War II, ServiceMaster Industries, Inc. was founded. Dominated by Christian men, the company grew from a small enterprise dispensing rug and furniture cleaning materials, as well as services for cleaning carpets and furniture in homes and business establishments, to a multiservice company grossing more than 500 million dollars by 1981, a third of a century after its founding. ServiceMaster's largest division provides a service to hospitals and rest homes in a number of countries. Thousands of employees are engaged in doing everything from providing food services to polishing floors. The company has recorded remarkable growth. Revenues have climbed at about 100 million each year for several years and will likely top a billion dollars within four years from its half billion achievement year.

ServiceMaster openly publishes and often reiterates its four great purposes for the company:

1. to honor God in all we do;
2. to help people develop;
3. to pursue excellence; and
4. to grow profitably.

As a result of focusing and following the purposes of the company, the managers and workers appear to possess a family type relationship within the ranks of workers. Family concerns of the workers and managers are sensitively mentioned at company meetings. Wives and husbands often work together in assignments and all are invited to major company meetings and social gatherings. When a person is honored, the spouse is called upon to share the honor.

In a speech delivered in early 1982 to hundreds of management personnel at area meetings through the United States, Kenneth T. Wessner, chairman of the board of ServiceMaster, and C. William Pollard, president, presented the problem of tension between business for profit that uses people, and business for profit for the benefit of people. In the address reproduced in the annual report of the company for 1981, the ideals of ServiceMaster appear:

Marion Wade, the founder of ServiceMaster . . . had a vision of a company committed to people, honoring God in their work and producing a standard of excellence in their service to others. . . . There is a growing belief among some people that a conflict exists between spiritual values on the one hand, and economic objectives on the other. Such people ask: Can there be anything in common between God and profit?

To understand worth, however, we must talk not about the value of things, but the value, the worth of people.

. . . Do we use people for production or production for people? . . . We must also ask whether the purposes and will of God are being accomplished in the process

(ServiceMaster Industries, Inc. 1981, 26-27).

Genuine Christian motivation is not the only reason for relating business and family as mutually identifiable social entities. In matter of fact, the melding of business and family perceptions may be more commonly perceived outside the western world than in. The Matsushita Electric Company of Japan is constructed along lines related to family concepts so that the family is set up to guide business rather than business principles guide the family. Matsushita manufactures Panasonic, Quasar, National and Technics products. It is one of the fifty largest corporations in the world (Pascale and Athos 1981, 37).

Matsushita openly relates company policies to family and cultural values, including religion. More than 200,000 employees are well instructed in the concepts. Some of the family perceptions include: (1) primary concern for people, with responsibility to two bosses (as children grow up responsible to two parents, mother and father); (2) organizational shifts back and forth between centralized and decentralized patterns (as they "swing back and forth in an ever more complex marriage"); (3) finance controllers who exert influence in the company (as "a wife in a traditional Japanese household"); and (4) dispute settlements within the company ("like husbands and wives do in a healthy marriage"). (Pascale and Athos 1981, 46, 58, 70) Matsushita, like a family has a humane system for instituting company discipline, for making a place for each and every employee, for providing participation with modest but widespread reward systems, for encouraging education and loyalty, and for stimulating self-esteem.

It is with perceptions of business companies like ServiceMaster and Matsushita that we relate here to family management. It would be as well to say that family perceptions are constructed into these business management patterns.

To be successful, managers coordinate meaningful factors related to their businesses. A business must provide a quality service or product to consumers at a reasonable price that will more than offset the cost of production. In formal business this process includes management of basic resources, property, production, labor, transportation, marketing, sales and research. Although the task of management is complex, especially as it relates to persons, principally laborers and consumers, the issues of management are understandable. The problems are soluble. Each effective business develops its strategy, structure and system within the restrictions of the style, skills and staff that it builds or cultivates.

Family Relates to Persons

A family is an "incorporation" of its membership. Membership is generally gained by marriage or blood. Casual or legal adoption is, of course, a legitimate means of entry. Members care for themselves and for one another whenever they can. When help is needed by mate, or child, or any person admitted by family extension, one or more family members assist, or ought to, until the individual is able to function on his own. There is high social and "business" efficiency in the plan. Jane Howard observed, lived with and participated in the activities of a number of families. She reported her experiences, observations and conclusion in her book, *Families.* She found that good families tended to reflect the same characteristics. The list includes: (1) a strong figure around whom the family clustered, (2) an archivist or historian who would keep scrapbooks and photo albums, (3) an atmosphere of continual busyness, (4) an ability to deal directly with trouble (problem solving), and (5) a sense of affection, ritual and place (Howard 1978, 241-245).

The members of a family are the "customers" of each other, consumers of family productivity and corporate services. The analogy also holds that every member should, as soon as possible, contribute or produce as well as consume. Depending on family circumstances, emphasis shifts back and forth from each member as consumer to each as provider. What attitudes should family members hold and display—both as consumers or beneficiaries of services and as contributors or providers of services?

Work and Worth

A parent laboring at a distance from home should be conscious of the family members—his duty to them as well as his pleasure in them. Such awareness reveals a holistic concept of all that the family is and is accomplishing. The attitude toward work is enhanced when the worker senses a job relationship to his or her family. The love or hate a person feels for his occupation may be, and sometimes is, translated by family members as love or hate for them. Certainly the attitude of the receiver as well as the giver contributes important interpretation to both for any life experience involving them.

Family members also evaluate the worth of what a parent does in his occupation by his attitude toward them. That attitude reveals his respect for them, which in turn creates a special relationship between them. They will certainly appreciate his work more if they understand the relationship of their family's welfare to his labor. But they sometimes do not. Judges note that a high percentage of troubled youths appearing before them do not know their fathers' or mothers' occupations.

Respect and Behavior

We believe then that attitudes toward outside work and its meaning affect concepts of a family member's worth in that member. Actions and attitudes within the family group also generate worth concepts. Our concern is for right and helpful concepts. How can they be generated? There are acceptable, appropriate ways for treating or relating to any and all persons. Human beings are not machines to be manipulated, are not punching bags to be pummeled, are not animals to be commanded, are not ordinary objects to be ignored. They are living, thinking, feeling, striving, developing human beings. Sometimes, of course, they become harsh, violent, crude, abusive and surly. One wonders how more considerate treatment during their formative years would have changed them. But we know negative approaches do not accomplish great good. We seek affirmations of ourselves and others.

Unless something occurs to distort their lives, citizens are expected to behave decently. To produce that behavior, they will need love, discipline, education, religion, nurture and opportunity, developed with virtues that these words imply. Children, and sometimes ill and aged adults, need "parenting" duties performed in their lives, preferably with gentle and sensitive hands, attitudes, voices. It has been said: To try to control a child by yelling at him is like driving an automobile by blowing its horn. An apt saying, often repeated, in our computerized age points out that "human beings are not to be folded, mutilated or spindled." They are to be treated as persons, which is to say, with respect.

When family members treat each other with respect as proper agents of love, care and concern, they gain balance between the corporate good of the family and the individual good of each of its members. In a family where individual members are respected, those individuals will, as a rule, cheerfully sublimate some of their personal desires for family benefit. And the family sometimes focuses on the individual. A birthday, a wedding, an illness, and the like are situations in point. Family issues are the issues of the one and the many. With awareness of persons each family member can learn and appreciate the beauty of his place in service. He serves and is the beneficiary of service.

Reading Related to Persons

Authors with Christian or generally Christian emphases:

Ahlem, Lloyd H. *Do I Have To Be Me?* Glendale, Calif.:
   Regal, 1973.
Bustanoby, Andre. *You Can Change Your Personality.*
   Grand Rapids: Zondervan, 1977.
Clinebell, Howard J., Jr. and Charlotte H. Clinebell. *The
   Intimate Marriage.* New York: Harper & Row, 1970.
Dobson, James. *What Wives Wish Their Husbands Knew
   About Women.* Wheaton, Ill.: Tyndale, 1975.
Guernsey, Dennis. *If I'm So Free How Come I Feel Boxed
   In?* Waco, Tex.: Word, 1978. (Chapters 1 and 2.)
Lee, Mark W. *Creative Christian Marriage.* Glendale,
   Calif.: Regal, 1977. (pp. 115-27.)
Lee, Mark W. *Who Am I and What Am I Doing Here?*
   Milford, Mich.: Mott Media, 1982.
Tournier, Paul. *The Meaning of Persons.* New York:
   Harper & Row, 1957.

Authors with secular or generally secular emphases:

Goldstine, Daniel. *The Dance-Away Lover.* New York:
   William Morrow, 1977.
Pascale, Richard Tanner and Anthony G. Athos. *The Art of
   Japanese Management.* New York: Simon & Schuster,
   1981.

CHAPTER 2

Motivation

- **Why do laborers do their work?**

- **What motivates family members?**

And whosoever will be chief among you, let him be your servant (Matt. 20:37).

But he that is greatest among you shall be your servant (Matt. 23:11).

Jesus said that he who would be greatest among His disciples should be the servant of all. This principle of servanthood is central to any discipleship, and our Lord repeated it in various ways so that its character could not be missed. The parable of the Good Samaritan, the offering of a cup of cold water to a thirsty man, the extra mile given by choice, and other biblical narratives are pointers to the way of a servant. The scriptural ideal is that Christians should outdo one another in service.

Motivating Factors in the Scriptures

Followers of Jesus are provided several strong word pictures about servanthood. Himself a model, Jesus is sometimes called "the Suffering Servant." He reminded His disciples that He served the will of His Father. And He shocked them when He took the role of a slave to wash their feet. During the Upper Room experience, and following the washing of the disciples' feet, Jesus used the slave analogy with His men (John 13). Slavery would be as repugnant to those Jews, remembering both their Egyptian period of history and their role as God's free children, as it would be to any privileged people freed from bondage. But a spiritually proud Jew, Saul of Tarsus who became Paul the apostle, felt himself to be a servant and represented himself as a bond slave to Jesus Christ. He did so not only for the love he had for Christ but for the purpose of ministry or service to mankind for the Lord's sake. Servanthood and humility ought to be characteristic of man.

Nevertheless, there is appealing moderation of the slavery concept in Scripture. Service, even spiritual service, carries its rewards. These are not only the intrinsic rewards of truth and virtue, but also particular benefits and, ultimately, even measurable ones. They include eventual heaven, immortality, wealth, authority and bliss. Paradise itself offers multiple rewards, including status, a special relationship with Jesus Christ. Apparently reward is in the order of things, both in nature and beyond. The person of faith waits for his reward.

Certainly, there are other motivating factors than servanthood in the Bible, but our emphasis, for the family, is in the principle of service. With that accent we limit our scope for the purpose of this chapter.

Motivating Factors in Business

Reward is important to business processes and success. Through various incentives, owners or managers motivate their workers to produce in sufficient volume to maintain their businesses. Enterprises that flourish are important for the welfare of their workers as well as for owners. Both owners and laborers feel they want to participate in these business ventures and will be proud of them.

Incentive Factors

How to reward and motivate employees is a principal concern for any company. Reward is more than monetary considerations such as salaries, wages or profits. In many management-labor negotiations, however, it often seems that money is nearly the whole of the reward. Money incentives are overemphasized during some historical cycles. When this happens, many human beings become too materialistic. But *salaries or wages* cannot be left out as incentive. While lust for money is an ever-present danger, money is a tool to be used for the good of one's business, one's family and others. It is even a tool for God's service. Mature persons find satisfactory balance in their attitudes relative to affluence.

Motivation, or stimulating people to work at accomplishing goals, is a major concern for managers. There are, however, several significant incentive factors besides money available. *Status* is one. A manager knows that a worker assigned an area of responsibility to control or supervise will likely feel his importance to the enterprise. An attractive and suitable title to go with responsibility enhances assignments. The worker feels, in professional situations, that he is more than a cipher, or than just one more person in a crowd. This is especially the case when the worker is given total responsibility for the whole assignment.

Appreciation is another motivator. When appreciation and genuine approval are demonstrated to a laborer, he will work harder and longer to maintain his reputation. Superior workers do not wish to be taken for granted, do not believe that the only reward accruing to them is in a paycheck. If there is nothing returned except money, the laborer will feel that recognition has been denied him. He needs to be thanked. Pascale and Athos refer to the supportive conduct in the Matsushita company:

> Praise and reinforcement are an important part of the Matsushita philosophy. In 1979, Matsushita received over 25 suggestions per employee. . . . Monetary and group rewards are given. Approximately 90% of these suggestions receive rewards . . . (Pascale and Athos 1981, 81-82).

Accomplishment also assists the worker to gain respect

for his own ability and experience. It is normal for a person to wish to do something well. All testimonies of champions and record-setters include statements about the euphoria they experience in their achievements. They feel power and gratification, as well as an awareness of personal worth. Acknowledging accomplishment is commonly called *recognition*. If recognition gets out of hand, of course, the human ego exceeds itself. Adulation and the desire for it becomes saccharin and false. Our concern here is with appropriate motivation.

There are other motivators, of course, like *love*, or *duty*, or *loyalty*, or *habit*, and these are legitimate, even virtuous, when in balance with other factors. They belong in both institutional and interpersonal relationships. In different people and circumstances they will exert varying amounts of emotional influence.

Psychic Income

There are many professional fields in which *psychic income* is, or has been, well recognized. Two of these, teaching and ministering, have commonly been referred to as professions in which rewards for the worker are sometimes found in the success of his students, or the spiritual growth of his parishioners, or some other personal gratification.

During much of history salary levels have been low for serving professions. Mothers devoting their lives to nurturing their children and caring for their husbands are seldom paid money. For generations teachers, ministers, and even government employees were paid at levels dramatically lower than were persons working in profitable industry. It was assumed that service employment, especially if it was public (tax supported) or in nonprofit institutions, was not to be rewarded in the same way as that which resulted in a profitable product or profession. During recent decades this viewpoint has been effectively challenged by service personnel. For example, unions of teachers, unions once believed unthinkable, have successfully closed down schools and forced financial and other improvements for instructors. Service industries currently compete well on the salary levels of other laborers and professionals.

Rising salaries and the accompanying decline of other rewards, like psychic income, have overemphasized money rewards and underemphasized others. But the laborer refuses to give up these other rewards. Once he is well paid, the wage earner expects recognition—the psychic rewards of status and appreciation. Those who are in service industries or who serve without standard monetary rewards deserve these other rewards even more.

Society seems ambivalent on this issue. Lip service is commonly given to an affirmation that "the best things in life are free." But, in fact, money and what it can do have become so important to the general society that the benefits of volunteerism, acts of loving and caring untouched by monetary considerations, have been denigrated. One wonders what virtue has been lost in a society that attaches a monetary price to everything. More needs to be done in our time to enhance the psychic motivators in industry, in family life—and in public life, too, for that matter.

During his tenure as governor of the state of California, Edmund G. Brown, Jr., argued that the employees of government—any government—holding the higher offices, should not expect lucrative salaries. For a time he resisted salary raises for those in upper echelons. He refused a mansion built for the governor and continued to drive his old Plymouth. His rationale was partly related to the fact that high-ranking public servants receive honors from other workers and society, honors both motivating and rewarding. Because these benefits were not present in the same degree in laboring and low status jobs, workers would have to be paid more, and the high status professionals not so much more. However, Brown's views did not attract many followers.

Service Rewards

Like the professions, industry needs similar motivation, unrelated to wages and profits. The quality of the service or product, pride in what is done, and satisfaction of consumers deserve prime business and life consideration. Proof of their importance may be found in the policies adopted by a company: in responding to complaints, in the prompt effectiveness of service departments, in the integrity of guarantees, and the like.

The late Conrad Hilton became wealthy by applying his aphorism: "The customer is always right." His premise became the motto of his hotel chain. No question was to be raised by any hotel employee about the justice of a claim. A guest, even if he could be proved wrong, was to be treated *as though* he could not be wrong. For Hilton, no explanations from patrons of his hotels were needed or expected. In an era following World War II, when hotels were closing because of poor management and competition from motels, Hilton constructed new, large hotels, and they flourished around the world.

The principle of unquestioned service is observed in other businesses. Sears, Roebuck and Co. has long relied on a variation of the "customer is right" theme. The Sears motto is: "Satisfaction guaranteed." Any product purchased from Sears is supposed to meet not only the guarantee of the manufacturer but the expectations of the purchaser. On occasion company managers have invited experts to instruct them on how to persuade employees to make good on the motto: "Satisfaction guaranteed." They have found that clerks sometimes reject returned merchandise because the merchandise had been used for a lengthy period, or the product was never designed to do what the customer insisted it should do, or the customer was chronic in taking items out and returning them without planning sensibly for his needs. But the motto has nothing to do with any rationale of justice. "Satisfaction guaranteed" means just that, regardless of the injustice of a claim. Management holds that any loss to the company on a transaction will be compensated by business increases stemming from customer belief that purchasing a product from Sears means that the buyer will be recompensed on request. Sales personnel are not easily persuaded that the simple guarantee is to be honored without question. They commonly insist on fairness for the company.

This emphasis on the customer as one to be served is seen also in salesmanship. Courses in salesmanship often accent simple basics in polite social exchange. Anyone who has worked in business fields has observed, even admired, the manners of effective businessmen/salesmen, and has been turned away by insincere, ineffective personnel. Even if I am interested in a product, I may not purchase it if the salesman has a harsh voice, disregards my person, uses crude language, imposes himself too far into my personal space, or violates my rights as I perceive them. I may shy from him if he even unconsciously assumes superiority or acts in self-centered ways. I have avoided salesmen who swear, who blow smoke toward me, who assume I am stupid or unfeeling because I am not purchasing their products at the moment.

A salesperson will do better to question his own attitudes and skills than the intractability of a potential customer. That potential customer holds the right to respond as he wishes, or to offer alternatives to any proposal. And he has the right, even an obligation in some instances, to refuse without explaining his position. All should be done within a context of mutual respect between the servant (salesperson) and the recipient (potential buyer).

A basic problem for those who make the laborer and the customer mere factors in business is that they neither improve business nor society for the long historical pull. Such a view of man, state Pascale and Athos, has had "revolutionary implications for the Western view of humankind. Humans (the labor content) were no longer an inextricable part of the whole of society. Rather, the person, as laborer, became an objectified and standardized compo-

nent of the production process. Not surprisingly, this
view of 'labor' tended to divorce man as a social and spiritual being from his 'productive' role at work" (Pascale
and Athos 1981, 29).

The authors rightly feel that the loss of social and spiritual meaning from people in their work is in error, costly to
business and society—and the family. The concept of business that is biblical, a concept followed by the church during many centuries, was challenged by Machiavelli in the
sixteenth century. He proposed management to be a
separate function from moral law. His amoral theory violated, and continues to violate the meaning of man and
family. We turn to moral foundations for business and
family—and for all social behavior or institutions. For the
Christian, all motives are filtered through biblical precepts.

Motivating Factors in the Family

Within the family, members also need to recognize the
elements that lead to acceptable types of behavior. They
seek high causes for action. Alertness to the family's needs
and expectations, to its concerns and problems, and to
quality of life show that family unity and cohesiveness are
not based exclusively on financial factors. Demonstrated
love, appreciation and confidence increase the overall
treasure of the family. These real virtues add to the emotional and psychological capital available to be invested
in the family or in others.

Psychic Rewards

How may the psychic motivations be made meaningful
in a family? Perhaps the most important factor is *awareness*. We must become aware of human need for recognition. We should provide opportunities where these
factors may operate. A home does well that: assigns one of
the children the position of director of clean-up each week,
praises a son who just cut the lawn, negotiates a special
privilege in turn for completion of a chore, sets aside a few

private minutes when a parent focuses total attention on a child, offers a well-worded compliment for a meal well-prepared, acknowledges a carefully groomed child, sings a song of love to another member of the family, brings a surprise to the one with the birthday, gives a rose to mother, rubs a sore back, tells a joke to the family, watches a television program with one or more children, takes a daughter to lunch, attends church together, reads a story from a book (perhaps a Bible story), touches son and daughter in loving gesture, and so the list grows. All these, and much more, are motivators. And they etch magnificent memories on our souls.

An addition to the previous list is the "allowance" counted out to each child on Saturday mornings. It is entirely appropriate, in a highly organized society, that each person should have independent use of his own money. This does not mean that a wife/mother is paid for housekeeping or child-rearing, but she should receive whatever amount is appropriate for recognition. Even a child, in the present world, must have at least something to manage on his own. To deny one family member the privilege of managing personal funds when another member does hold that privilege, is to disregard the right to privacy, to recognition, to self-expression. The total amount received by the person should not be related only to services performed. Money, no matter how small the amount, is as much a part of a person's life as clothing or furniture. Like clothing or furniture, money serves a need and enhances appropriately at least a little of the self-esteem of the person having and managing it.

Effective parenting also needs to be recognized in psychic rewards. For most parents those psychic returns are all they really desire. As parents, my wife and I are totally satisfied with our investment of time, money, love and all else that we gave to bearing and rearing children. We expect no financial reward, nor support from the government or any other agency. It would never occur to their mother that our children, or anyone else, should pay her a wage

for the investment she made in them or our home. Her gratification is complete, in that our sons and daughters lived
to maturity, are loving to God and parents, and pass on to
their children the heritage they received. The rewards, psychic income, are quite enough for us. We dare not put dollar values on what was done. The demands of some
advocates to place monetary value on homemaking and
child-rearing seem to us to degrade the idealism we place
on home and family.

The question naturally arises: Why may not a person receive all the monetary reward and the pyschic ones as
well? For reasons elusive to us, life does not work out that
way. When a product is fully paid for, or perceived to be,
with money, most of any other virtue is diluted in the
transaction. We should avoid becoming mere hirelings.
When parents are paid for rearing children, then shifting
responsibility to other adults, or near adults, who are also
paid, will seem to be appropriate and sufficient. These
others will be expected to do as parents would do, in exchange for a salary. It will become more difficult then to
maintain relationships based entirely on spiritual and human qualities like love, appreciation, selflessness and
virtue.

Self-Love Distorted

The human being rebels against service. "I hate house-
work." "I don't want to do that—it's too menial." "I am an
important person; that chore is beneath my dignity." Self-
centered complaints multiply. Examples from sports, entertainment, business, even academia, are commonplace illus-
trations of what has been called the new narcissism. Nar-
cissus, according to mythology, was infatuated by his own
reflection in the water and pined away because he could
not consummate self-love. One reviewer stated the case regarding the concern of Western society, and America in
particular, with the individual and the individual with
himself, this way:

Narcissism may not be a constant or universal disorder, but it is hard to deny that the horizons of millions of Americans have become the limits of themselves. Perhaps that has always been true, but not with so much legitimacy (Sheppard 1979, 77).

Counselors are often faced, in dealing with troubled married couples, with an overpowering self-love manifested by one or the other, or by both mates. Sometimes they protest their "rights" or assert the discovery of a new "awareness." They believe these grounds justify abandonment and divorce. Duty, love for others, self-sacrifice, and sensitivity to the future are presumed to be evils. The "discoveries" leave children and mate, as well as other family members, in shock and disappointment.

The lengthy, slow, somewhat undramatic withdrawal of many husbands/fathers from the family during most of the twentieth century has been joined, in most recent decades, by the dramatic withdrawal of many wives/mothers in what is sometimes touted as the "liberation movement." It is understood that not all "liberated" males and females, nor all liberationists, eschew the servant philosophy of life and duty. However, self-centered preoccupation among a-moral males and female liberationists gains major publicity. That publicity guides later performances of impressionable new members of society.

A dramatic illustration of this self-centeredness is found in the arguments advanced by former wives and mothers who have become lesbians. These mothers firmly allege their rights to keep and rear children in a home where two adult women, in sexual liaison with one another, presume to replace traditional father and mother roles.

How does parental egocentrism affect the children? Most family counselors feel that this preoccupation by mother, father and sometimes another family member commonly causes extensive personal problems for children. Intense parental self-interest is likely to affect children adversely. Certainly some children are more competent to cope than

others. But as the final years of the twentieth century
appear, parental failure may become the most serious of
all social problems.

The late Philip Wylie, a secular writer on social themes,
asserted that "Pop is a moral slacker." He also attacked the
parenthood failure of mothers. "Momism," he termed it.
Some of his analyses occurred before the urban problems
of parenting became widely recognized. Wylie believed that
money-making by men does not assure their talents for fa-
thering, and smothering by women does not mean
mothering. He appeared to believe that parents had failed
to do their duty in a society dominated by urbanization
and affluence. Many adults no longer were willing to sacrifice energy and time to nurturing children. In an urban society children have become bothersome.

Preoccupation with self is foreign to the Christian concept of family. In the Christian scheme, self is partly
denied for the sake of others. Sometimes one is called on
for self-denial, insofar as that is possible. Awareness that
rearing children presumes some self-denial for parents is
part of the reason many couples avoid generation of children. At least these adults are reluctant to visit their self-
preoccupation or interests on children who might, as a consequence, feel unwanted. The desire to bear children, a biological function and fulfillment, must be matched by a desire to parent, a psychological and spiritual function which
ought to be fulfilling. The two desires may not be simul-
taneous for many people. In this differential there is tragedy for many couples and children.

Resistance to Service

The "Peter protest," as someone has dubbed the term, explains some Christians in their self-centeredness. The story
is well-known: Jesus removed His clothing, girded himself
with a towel and proceeded to wash His disciples' feet.
Peter protested, "You will not wash my feet." Peter knew
that if Jesus served him, then he, Peter, would be logically
and morally bound to serve others. If a superior serves an

inferior (the greater serving the lesser), then the lesser must serve not only his superior, but his peers and less than peers. To accept the legitimacy of Jesus' service to disciples, and in particular to Peter, meant that he, Peter, must become the servant of all others. By the time of Pentecost, Peter had learned and accepted the principle. Judas rejected it outright.

Protests, common in our time, against servant roles violate the Christian's purpose. They deny Scripture. Spouses are supposed to serve each other and their children as well. Our children should learn about servant roles they should adopt, and should be encouraged to practice them early in life until they master those patterns.

The duties of a husband/father role are summarized in God's commandment to the father—to love. The duties of a wife/mother role are summarized in God's commandment to the mother—to submit. The duties of a child role are summarized in God's commandment to the child—to be obedient (Col. 3:18-20). Each of these commandments followed to its conclusion leads to servanthood. One is not easier, nor more demeaning, than the other. All lead to damping, without destroying, self-interest, for the purpose of serving others—principally those of one's own household.

There is a kind of self-interest in service, in that those who serve are more likely to be served by their beneficiaries when appropriate need arises. This servanthood role may be easier to follow if one is the object, the beneficiary, of the service of others in something of an even exchange. Give some, take some. It is the reciprocal principle that is fair and equitable. But the Christian principle, which does not totally set aside reciprocity, does not rely on it. Servanthood applies even if it is one-sided, and even if one must do all the giving. If this were not true, passages like 1 Corinthians 13 would lose their meaning.

The members of my family are my first objects of service. For me that service is not meant to generate personal pride, or stimulate special expectations for myself, or turn a profit. However, I hope for some appreciation, some affection, some cooperation. In any event, my service is not, or should not be, dependent on anything except the motivation to serve God as prescribed in the Scriptures. How this is done is perfectly modeled in Christ. His concern for individuals, for His disciples, for the masses, models conduct for me. That example is applied initially in my family. Mastering the process there, I may succeed with other persons outside my little circle.

Practicing Amenities

Perhaps families ought to begin with a basic rule of business—be polite. There is a standard of good manners that may not be as widely followed as we might wish, but the standard remains. We appreciate and admire that standard when we observe and register its practice. Some persons do wait for others to go first, do say "please," or "thank you," or "you're welcome." They do permit statements to be made without interruption. They are gracious. They do respect time frames. They do not see chivalrous conduct as demeaning either to the one performing the act or the one receiving it. Gracious living as an attitude belongs to all persons, even those in modest circumstances. It is important to developing family dignity.

A husband and wife who are considerate of each other will together establish a home atmosphere that is positive. Through their conduct, parents present models in casual home behavior by which children may learn to act in appropriate ways. They will begin to act graciously as matter of course. As they respond to such instruction, sibling rivalry will be reduced, and younger members of the family will sense something of gentle and cultured attitudes. An aura of graciousness is created.

Part of the alleged solution to the cost of family caring is for individuals to move toward a single lifestyle. Each person takes charge of himself, and is casual to serve as he wishes. This book opened by acknowledging the complexity of modern family life. An excess in complexity has been generated, and is not really necessary. Matters

could be simplified somewhat. Relationships in intimacy
are worth the investment we give to them. If persons stop
holding out until material and other rewards are increased
for themselves, we may expect satisfaction in other ways
for individuals and families. There are and must be rewards, but we remind ourselves about William James's observation that lives based on *having* are less free than
those based on *doing* or *being.*

Perhaps we should be concerned with imbalances in us
rather than in the rewards themselves. My wife presented
me with four children, two sons and two daughters. We
perceived them as little persons and treated them cour-
teously, insisting they respond in a similar manner to us
and to each other. I believe we faced our duty to rear them,
nurture them, and guide them to maturity. The statements
they make as adults arouse within us a feeling that we
performed our tasks to their, and our, general satisfaction.
Our relationships with them and our grandchildren are
gratifying. And when we observe exchanges between them,
even during stressful times and personal differences, we
are impressed with the respectful manners they use with
each other.

Even with that gratifying perception of our present and
former relationships with our children, I would shift somewhat my own approach if my parenting days were to be
relived. I would find ways to demonstrate more fully the
sensitivity I felt. There would be fewer excuses for busy
times, for preoccupations, for duties and weariness.

If the period were to be lived again, I would give more
time to my primary "customers." I would have held them
more, talked to them more, walked with them more, sung
to them more, wrestled with them more, laughed with them
more, attended ball games with them more—and so on.
Others, the secondary "customers," would have received
less of my attention. And that does not mean I would have
neglected the second line of privilege and duty. The secondaries were sometimes treated as primaries, when they
should have remained secondaries. They would have been

appropriately served, albeit on an adjusted schedule.

For inexplicable reasons, human beings are often at their best with strangers, to those who window-shop in our lives, or who may buy no more than a trinket from our store of life. The real buyers—spouse and children—must wait. For these the store may be seldom open. Closing time shuts them out. There is an old aphorism that fits the point: "All the children have shoes except the shoemaker's."

Of course each of us has only so much to give. On a particular day it may all be given out to others rather than our own family members. Some of those others do not care for our help to the degree family members do, or would. But the shop is closed. The owner—the leader or parent or other family member—must work on his own recuperation.

To be a family member, in the best sense, is to be a servant. The best servant serves, with a sense of proper priorities, those closest to him, those he is responsible to serve first, then second, then last. The more thorough and mature his service, the more that member can teach servanthood effectively to other members. When he does so model and teach, he models and teaches as Christ did.

Reading Related to Motivation

Authors with Christian or generally Christian emphases:

Dobson, James. *Dare to Discipline.*Wheaton, Ill.:
  Tyndale, 1977.
Goddard, Hazel B. *I've Got That Hopeless, Caged-In
  Feeling.* Wheaton, Ill.: Tyndale, 1971. (Chap. 7: "The
  Healing of Families.")
Lee, Mark W. *How To Have A Good Marriage.* Chappaqua,
  N.Y.: Christian Herald, 1978. ("What Do You Both Know
  About Your Temperaments?" pp. 69-71.)
LeTourneau, Richard. *Management Plus.* Grand Rapids,
  Mich.: Zondervan Publishing House, 1973.
Petersen, J. Allan. *For Men Only.* Wheaton, Ill.: Tyndale,
  1973. (Chap. 1, pp. 15-51.)

Authors with secular or generally secular emphases:

Baird, John E. *The Dynamics of Organizational Communi-
  cation.* New York: Harper & Row, 1977.
Eimers, Robert and Robert Aitchison. *Effective Parents:
  Responsible Children.* New York: McGraw-Hill, 1977.
  (Chap. 8: "Special Incentive Programs.")
Elgin, Duane. *Voluntary Simplicity.* New York: William
  Morrow, 1981.

CHAPTER **3**

Identity

- **What business is this, and how shall it be identified?**

- **How do family and home relate to personal identity?**

And she shall bring forth a son, and thou shalt call his name JESUS: for he shall save his people from their sins (Matt. 1:21).

Behold a virgin shall be with child, and shall bring forth a son, and they shall call his name Emmanuel, which being interpreted is, God with us (Matt. 1:23).

And when they were come into the house, they saw the young child with Mary his mother, and fell down, and worshipped him: and when they had opened their treasures, they presented unto him gifts; gold, and frankincense, and myrrh (Matt. 2:11).

When Jesus therefore saw his mother, and the disciple standing by, whom he loved, he saith unto his mother, Woman, behold thy son! Then saith he to the disciple, Behold thy mother! And from that hour that disciple took her unto his own home (John 19:26-27).

The importance of naming and the names themselves in man's historical tradition instruct us in some way even in modern times. Certainly the Scriptures attach importance to names as vital to perceptions of ancient culture. When a person or circumstances changed, names were often changed. Abram became Abraham. Sarai became Sarah. Isaac, "laughter," represented the experience of his mother Sarah in response to the promise of a child of her own at her advanced age. The story of names and naming is a major biblical one.

Identity in the Scriptures

On occasion change in character or commitment in the Bible meant change in name. Jacob demanded the name of the wrestling angel and was himself given a new name, Israel. Jacob then changed the name of the place where his own name was changed. Commonly a pattern was followed that made names meaningful in tribal Israel as in most of the ancient world.

John the Baptist was dedicated by his parents with a name different from that of his father or any known ancestor (Luke 1:59-63). Friends believed the infant would be given a family name, in honor of ancestry. Struck dumb for John's gestation period, Zacharias verified in writing his wife's declaration: *His name shall be called John.* Immediately Zacharias regained his lost speech. And from that moment John began the experience of becoming John, and later, John the Baptist. Ultimately his name identified his ministry—he was a baptizer.

As implied in the verses opening this chapter, the names of Jesus provide an interesting study in meaning: *Thou shalt call his name Jesus, for he shall save his people from their sins.* It was by so great a goal, salvation, that the name of the Savior was chosen. Isaiah suggested other names for Him: Wonderful Counselor, Mighty God, Prince of Peace (9:6) and Immanuel, God with Us (7:14). Prophets and poets called Him "the righteous Branch" (Jer. 23:5) and the "lamb" (Isa. 53:7). Names for God occupy a section of any complete work in systematic theology. Special works have been written about the names for God and the effect of those names on man.

Throughout the Scriptures, as already noted, the names of persons, places and things have meaning. Adam (man),

Abram (father) changed to Abraham (father of a multitude), Isaac (laughter), Jacob (heel grabber) changed to Israel (he will rule as God), and others represent the importance and meaning of names as teaching devices. The most dramatic is the name of Jesus (Savior), and Jesus Christ (anointed Savior). This uniqueness of the anointed Savior was acknowledged by the Apostle Peter who was Cephas (a stone or pebble) renamed by Jesus as Peter (a rock). When Jacob was blessed at Luz, he renamed the place Bethel (house of God). And when God was perceived to have accomplished His work in some marvelous way, the recipient might coin another name for God, such as Jehovah-jireh (God will provide); or Gideon's Jehovah-shalom (Jehovah is peace); or Moses' Jehovah-nissi (the Lord is my banner).

House and Home

Closely related to names are identities of events in the life of an individual (Benjamin) or his character (Nabal), or his circumstances (Ichabod), or the place of his ancestry or birth (Judas Iscariot). Jesus' ancestry was from Bethlehem (the house of David), but He was known to be the Nazarene from Nazareth (the home of Joseph and Mary). Two of the Scripture references at the beginning of this chapter refer to house and to home. The first relates to events at the time of the birth of Jesus, and the second to the time of His death. The implications found in the passages arouse our imaginations.

In the first, the reference is to a house, undoubtedly borrowed or rented, to which Joseph took Mary and the infant Jesus. Details on personal family matters are wholly missing. The day after Jesus' birth must have occupied Joseph in the search for improved lodgings from the stable. We are not told what his feelings were. He may have been angered at what happened, or perhaps he was embarrassed, feeling he had handled matters clumsily for Mary in her condition. On that very day he may have located a house, perhaps one that belonged to relatives. His skills would put it in order, at least the part needed for the care of mother and child. At worst, in a matter of a few days after Jesus' birth the family was relatively comfortable and independent. But the point is made. The husband, mother and child needed a house, and they had it. The unusual events of the birth night at the inn and stable were quickly and mercifully ended. Order was needed, and Joseph provided it. To this house, some weeks later, the wealthy Eastern magi came. Their gifts, in some part, provided means for meeting living costs for Joseph, who was likely at work plying his carpentry trade. Bethlehem citizens at the time would relate Jesus more to this house in their neighborhood than to the manger we remember.

The second reference implies the solidarity of home and family. Jesus, eldest son of Mary, was perceived to be her protector after Joseph's death which must have occurred some years earlier. During His ministry He was called on to deal with family matters from time to time. Among the concerns of Jesus during His dying hours was His mother. In keeping with His duty to care for her, Jesus requested from the cross that the disciple John accept the responsibility and that Mary accept the substitution. Apparently both John and Mary immediately received the directive as loving and appropriate. Before the end of the ordeal of Jesus, John escorted Mary to his own *home*. The meaning appears to relate to the solidarity, safety, and compassion gained when one is at home.

Reading the Scriptures perceptively, one is impressed by the centrality of the home in the lives of people. Commonly, Jesus stayed in the homes of people, teaching or resting in them. Jesus ate with people at their tables and discussed their situations. The apostles appear to have followed a similar pattern. Many churches founded in various cities on missionary routes, in ancient and modern times, were begun in homes.

Jesus used home and family in His teachings. When the prodigal came to the end of himself, he went home. The implication holds that no other place would be as idyllic as

his father's home. The father, analogous to the Heavenly
Father, was ideally presented in the environment of his
home. The lesson ought to be as clear and appealing to
moderns as it was to ancients.

Each of us should have a home. If we do not have one, or
cannot return to our parental home, we can make one, not
only for ourselves but for others who could be at home
with us. The important matter is to create a home that contributes to our identity. Does my home help me to become
the person I ought to become? Is it ordered in such a way
that those who observe it, and the life of my family in it,
register the witness of that home?

Identity in Business

A business has its own identity. An awareness of the
identity of an institution precedes any general acceptance
of that institution.

For a business, identity is discovered and communicated
in a number of ways. Identity is usually established by the
founders of the business. If it is not, the business may
soon fail or may function at lower levels of achievement
than efficiency analysts would approve. Businesses often
flounder because they are poorly conceived and developed.
They have no clear identity. Although much could be
learned by reviewing business failure caused by identity
crises in companies, our concern in this writing is with
factors that characterize successful institutions.

A business should be sufficiently concerned with identity to make sure its image is developed through every legitimate means. Everything chosen to represent institution
identity—colors, stationery, logo, photography, grooming
for employees—are matters for lengthy discussion and decision. When Bell Telephone Company committed its
graphics creation to an agency, the agency began its work
by studying the history of the company, its administration,
future purposes, and day-by-day functions. When careful
investigation was complete, a proposal was conceived and
formulated: the colors selected were blue, yellow and white

(to be used in carefully prescribed ways). The logo was a bell in a circle to express in instant visual form the purpose of the company. Identity of the company was also incorporated in the office stationery, the paint on the trucks, the uniforms of the repair personnel, and the like. Through a coordinated plan, Bell Telephone caused outside citizens to recognize the company easily.

Also important to business identity is its geographical location. A business establishes a home office, the center of its authority. This is its physical heart, where responsible and authoritative persons are present and functioning. Here the general policies of the business are determined. Everything of importance to the image of the company, to the production of goods or services, to the welfare of employees, and the like is related to the home office. Whatever happens there affects all personnel related to the corporation, wherever they may be.

If an institution is well managed, it identifies itself to the public in standard ways. For example, awareness is reinforced through historical aids to identity. Churches use crosses, or stars, or architecture. Colleges use towers, mortar boards and initials. Airlines use wings, uniforms, colors and logos. Nations and states use flags, photographs and monograms. Identity systems seem endless. Alert persons observe and appreciate the identifying factors of the world of activity.

Businesses sometimes need homes as part of their identity. Bankers discovered, following World War II, that their customers were somewhat negative about the atmosphere in banks. Managers evaluated their buildings and furnishings. Environments in banks were found to be cold, forbidding, formal, sterile. Warmer environments were introduced and more cordial personnel were trained to serve the public. Homelike buildings were sometimes constructed in residential areas. Business boomed. The banker admittedly took a page from the "family" situation. Banks became family institutions, a concept A.P. Giannini had introduced in San Francisco at the turn of the twentieth cen-

tury. His idea, to appeal to the family, the small depositor,
made Bank of America the largest public bank in the
world. Current banking practices, for many large banks,
may not rely on the small depositor, but the place of family perceptions remain important for business success.

Identity in the Family

Perhaps the most common question of our time raised by
collegians and other young adults is: Who am I? It is a
question that may be unanswerable in the way questioners
demand an answer (Lee 1982, chap. 1). The mystery of
one's individuality is not easily translated into ideas satisfying to most individuals. The answers generally are not
the ones they wish to hear.

Nevertheless, some answers are available. For example,
an individual can find his spiritual self if he is attentive to
the matter, and that discovery affects all other personal
discoveries. Who am I, spiritually? The Scriptures define
human beings as sinners, troubled by constitutional problems that cripple them in nearly every way, including limited ability to understand themselves. Redemption
provided in the sacrifice of Jesus Christ is an important
factor in self-discovery. The Apostle Paul, Augustine, Mar-
tin Luther, and many other eminent historical Christian
figures who have written perceptively about their experiences, identify their salvation as the most influential factor contributing to self-discovery. If persons have lost their
identity, it must be primarily in spiritual perceptions. If
they find it again, it is spiritual identity they discover that
is most satisfying.

There are areas other than spiritual in which self-
discovery is or ought to be made. One of these is family. In
family several factors contribute inevitably to identity. My
mother and father gave me a name and by it contributed
something to the formation of whatever I have become.
They provided both hereditary and environmental influences. In these legitimate factors I found some belonging. They provided evidence about my biological

roots. I was where I was supposed to be, having sprung
from a family of generations.

I know myself in part by belonging to the father and
mother who generated me. Many persons who have been
adopted invest significant money and time looking for
their biological parents in order to "discover" who they
are in themselves. Most appear satisfied when their
human generation can be identified. But the issue is
larger than biology.

Eminent families once accented their identity and pride
in various ways. Centuries ago family colors were selected. A coat of arms was designed and struck to capture the
history and distinctives of the individual family or clan. A
motto was chosen and expressed in Latin or Greek.
Clothing or fabrics were selected to identify the family.
Whole peoples might follow the tradition as in choices of
tartans by Scottish clans. Family traditions were important and, for many, are continued.

Naming Aids Identification

The name given to each person by his parents ultimately identifies him in more ways than merely
segregating him from all other human beings. That name
may have accumulated honor or dishonor long before the
birth of this child. Perhaps the name is undistinguished
and unrecognized. Or the name may be so distinguished
that an heir to that name finds it impossible to live up to
expectations placed on him by his family or the public.

One way or another, a person's name affects its owner,
for good or ill. Some parents sacrifice potential favorable
chances for their children by making dismal jokes of their
names. A lad named Mickey Mouse received a letter of
condolence from a man named Donald Duck. Mr. Duck
acknowledged that the child would face problems because
of his name. It is not likely that these men, one *actually*
named Mickey Mouse and the other Donald Duck, will ever
be taken seriously for positions or offices they might have
won had their names been determined to permit emergence

of their own personalities rather than comic characters. In most instances of this nature the victims change their names, or use a middle name to hide the first.

A significant number of adults do change their names. And for good reason. My mother was her parents' first-born. Her father, a farmer, was determined that first child would be a son, and chose a suitable name, Clyde, for "him." God and biology gave a girl. My grandfather revealed his initial disappointment in naming my mother Clyde. When adult, she changed her name, retaining the original as her middle name, but using only the initial to identify it. Those who knew her as a child, including her brothers and sisters, continued to address her as Clyde. She is known, in her advanced years in the Georgia community where she was born, as "Miss Clyde." In her community that address, "Miss," is a sign of respect.

My mother's name was the middle name of Mr. Joyce Clyde Hall, founder, at nineteen years of age, of the company that became Hallmark Cards. Hall's obituary included the following:

> Hall was named after a Methodist bishop, Isaac W. Joyce and the name plagued him all his life. Even after he had achieved a degree of fame, he received letters addressed to "Miss" Joyce Hall. Interviewers seldom failed to ask how he liked being named Joyce.

> "I got used to it," he said. "Clyde . . . wasn't any great shakes of a name either" (San Francisco Chronicle, Oct. 30, 1982, p. 18).

Joseph Kennedy, patriarch of what is called the "Kennedy clan," reminded his children they were "Kennedys" with attitudes, style, service orientation, money, even religion that characterized them. Kennedy family tradition began in Ireland and part of it was transferred to the American home of immigrating members. New factors were added, like public service for family sons. "Honey

Fitz" Fitzgerald was a well-known Irish congressman from
Massachusetts, whose power was feared and respected.
From him John Fitzgerald Kennedy received his middle
name.

One might list names of historical and political person-
ages and note general responses to those names—Abraham
Lincoln, Franklin Roosevelt (or just FDR), Henry Ford, Albert Einstein. Other personal names hold significant meaning: Rockefeller, Edison, Tolstoy, Churchill, Hitler, Mar-
coni, Curie, Barnum, Moody, Graham, Pope John XXIII,
Lindbergh, MacArthur, and thousands of others represent-
ing eminent persons, living and dead. For knowledgeable
men and women each name calls back memory of
associates and members of the named person or family.
The name is key to a memory bank of material much larger
than the name itself.

What's in a Name?

In American and Canadian societies names are selected
for the most part without concern for meaning. Popularity
of certain names, or the euphony of them, or an unusual
shift in spelling, or masculine to feminine adaptations,
seem to dominate selections. Much may be lost for modern
families in that a child has no real commitment to meaning
in his name, something he can live up to. There is reason
to believe that this omission is a loss, perhaps small for
most, but nevertheless a loss in influence upon life. No one
knows how significant it is.

Anyone acquainted with motivational factors knows that
names make more than passing differences. Movie and
other entertainment people are careful to choose appealing
names to project images they wish to create. Engelbert
Humperdinck was a professional nothing, we are told, until he adopted the name "Engelbert Humperdinck." He sang
and performed the same way after fabricating his new
name as he had before. The name gained new attention and
changed his life. Later, with popular identity established,
he became simply, Engelbert. The change occurred during a

period when entertainers perceived themselves to be super-stars when they were recognized with one name: Cher, Ann-Margaret, Elvis.

Names make significant difference, even in longevity of life, if the observations of Trevor Weston, the British psychologist, are valid. He stated that in Great Britain those persons whose last names began with any of the eight last letters of the English alphabet made up the victims of "alphabetical neurosis." He found they had more ulcers, heart attacks, and mental problems, and died years earlier than persons whose names began with letters A through R. In *The Name Game,* the American author, Christopher Anderson, supported Weston's implications by studying the deaths of eminent persons during one year, all but one month of it in 1974. He discovered the early alphabet people averaged over 76 years of life and the last eight letter people, 68 years (Anderson 1977, 100-101).

According to Dr. Joyce Brothers, states Richard Pritchett, some first names of students, such as Elmer, Hubert or Bertha, attract lower grades from teachers than do other names, such as David, Michael, Lisa or Karen. And crime rates are four times higher among boys with unusual names than conventional ones (Pritchett 1978, 33).

Although we are often casual in naming and nicknaming our children, we ought to believe that the process deserves more care. One of my daughters-in-law was highly selective in names for her children. She named her daughter, Kyrsten, and her son, Jordan. Kyrsten was chosen to focus on the meaning, "the anointed," and also reflect, by its spelling, her maternal/paternal Scandinavian background. The spelling was chosen as a modified rendition of the way it would appear in Norwegian (Kjersten). That spelling might require more explanation than would be convenient when pronunciation and spelling were introduced in English conversation.

"Jordan" has two meanings: one attractive—"the sustainer," and one unattractive—"the crooked one." The River

Jordan winds its tortuous, "crooked" route from the Sea of Galilee to the Dead Sea. Obviously, the first meaning, "the sustainer," was the choice of his mother. She mildly regrets the second meaning exists. Also, in the selection of the word, Jordan, a bow was made to American popularity of euphony or sound. It is likely the names will affect positively the lives of these children, if they are used meaningfully with their parents or others and later in the intimacy of their own thoughts about themselves.

When asked if she used their names as motivation for the children to live up to implied ideals, their mother answered that it was more of a reminder for the parents to conduct themselves in ways that would be loving and respectful toward their children, whom they believed to be gifts from God. The names, when thoughtfully used, reminded them of that belief.

Personal Space and Identity

The concept of *personal space* is an important one. Personal space is often referred to as the six inches, or one, two or three feet of air, sometimes more, surrounding an individual. He is accompanied by this layer of space wherever he goes. He believes it belongs to him and should not be invaded. Family members and a few intimate friends may be invited to draw close. But commonly, personal space is guarded in some way, often unknowingly, by the person himself.

He even claims *territorial rights*. Territorial space is ultimately extended to a claim on the driver's seat in one's car, part of an office, side of the bed, or a particular pew in church. The individual feels he holds right to the few inches around his plate and chair as he sits at dinner. He is slightly unnerved if someone, without permission, sets a salt shaker or some other object within that territory. But no large area seems more territorial, more one's own, than his home.

Proper care and development of a house, apartment, mobile home, condominium, or whatever is called home,

becomes vital to the well-being of each individual in a
family. Each child should, if possible, have his own room
in his family home by the time he is in junior high school.
This is personal and territorial space within the larger territory. What is ours also becomes mine. The wife/mother
should have her kitchen, if she majors in homemaking, and
no one should invade it without permission or invitation.
Certainly she, like others staking claims, should be generous, but it is her territory if she stakes it out. The husband's handyman workshop should not be violated without
permission. (On some occasions it is the husband's kitchen
and the wife's workshop.) Each person has right to space,
and the intimate members of the family ought to respect
reasonable claims made for that space.

In this difficult balance between identity with others and
self-identity is the discovery of oneself. Much of life is
testing boundaries to find where one boundary begins and
the other ends. It is also making adjustments by moving
boundaries as one discovers himself and others. It is living, with adjustments, both alone and with intimate others.

Our family experienced a dramatic event when our first
child departed for college. Sharon, our eldest child, is ten
years senior to her sister, Jody, our youngest. They slept in
the same room and enjoyed a happy relationship. Sharon
was something of a second mother to her sister. (We did
not keep the suggestion noted above, that each child
should have his own room. Our home was not large
enough.)

When Sharon went to college, Jody seemed almost bereft
for several months, even though she saw her sister often.
The college was a half-mile distant from home. But that
made little difference. Jody did not wish to remain in the
room she had shared with her sister. She negotiated with
me to move my home study into her room, and she would
make what had served as my study her bedroom. So an exchange was made—a new life was begun. She made her
room over in her image. One of the things she did was to
locate her bed next to a large window. Watching the stars

during late evenings, she would sometimes describe her feelings to me. She made the room, but the room also made her. And what happened was good.

Home is a place where values may be effectively expressed. A man or woman is forced to be adaptable in public places or as a visitor on his neighbor's property. But here he may speak as he wishes, dress as he wishes, present the culture of his taste, and the like. Here he is most free. This place instructs a perceptive visitor about the resident's lifestyle, interests, and quality of life.

Home Environment

Environment is created in our homes as limited, personal environment. Factors are added, subtracted, even added again as we choose. These have to do with furniture, colors, books, hangings, room sizes, and whatever is included to make a house a home. If all factors seem normal to us, it is likely that we are comfortable, most like we want to be, somewhat confident in the home environment we create. Perhaps this feeling is on occasion lost for us, because we take environment for granted and do too little to maintain it at a satisfactory level. Housekeeping is neglected: the yard goes to seed.

Knowing their rights of possession, many family members believe their homes will maintain themselves. They do not. Housekeeping and gardening chores, neglected, create a different environment than would exist if they were completed. Choices of furnishings, art objects, appliances, colors are made by us or for us. Afterwards they play a role in forming us. Environment may even be spoiled by our various personal habits, including language and grooming styles.

If duties are disregarded, the home is to some degree dishonored or denigrated. Husbands spend less time in their homes when housekeeping is poorly done than they do when it is well done. As a rule, wives are happier in well-ordered homes than in disordered. However, if family members are overly meticulous, demonstrating their inflexibility, a home becomes sterile and cold.

Home Relates to Identity

A home is where a particular person may be found. A person by this name at this address is specified out of the billions of otherwise unidentified men and women in the world. This specificity seems almost magical. This "needle in the haystack" may be found with a little effort. The very exactness of the name and place intimates that my domicile has something to do with my identity.

Home is my own "turf." Something of me is there. I ought to be able to relax and feel good about myself in that place. The world from there ought to look better than it might from any other vantage point for me. If this is not true, it is because I am unacquainted with the meaning of *home*, or I have given nothing to it. Perhaps family members have in some way spoiled the place, making it unattractive for me. Perhaps I spoil it for myself and others. A house does not become a home without people in it, and the people relate meaningfully and specially, even spiritually, if the home maintains the full loyalty of its members.

Home is where my authority is greatest. Others outside my family, with higher status generally than I have, are humbled to my wishes when they stand with me in my own place. They are present by my permission, stated or implied. They defer to my rights on my territory. If the owner of the home chooses, he may put the visitor to disadvantage and embarrassment. Whatever power is intrinsic in the situation accrues to the occupant, the possessor of this place.

It is likely that persons of property feel better about themselves and understand themselves more than do those who possess nothing. Unless, of course, they choose personal lifestyles that give up property rights for other values important to them. We do know that a person tends to work harder when he cultivates "his own land." Production is higher on privately owned land than on state owned land, as a general rule.

His own corner can inform a man about himself, and others are told something about him. His home may reveal him to be a selfish person, one who shuts out others, family members or neighbors. Or it reveals his generosity and love. He is, in part, identified.

Reading Related to Identity

Authors with Christian or generally Christian emphases:

Ahlem, Lloyd H. *Do I Have To Be Me?* Glendale, Calif.:
    Regal, 1973.
Lee, Mark W. *Who Am I And What Am I Doing Here?*
    Milford, Mich.: Mott Media, 1982.
Myers, David G. *The Inflated Self.* New York:
    The Seabury Press, 1981.
Osborne, Cecil G. *The Art of Learning To Love Yourself.*
    Grand Rapids: Zondervan, 1982.
Sproul, R.C. *In Search of Dignity.* Ventura, Calif.:
    Regal Books, 1983.
Tournier, Paul. *The Meaning of Persons.* New York:
    Harper & Row, 1957.

Authors with secular or generally secular emphases:

Coopersmith, Stanley. *The Antecedents of Self-Esteem.*
    San Francisco: W.H. Freeman, 1967.
Lasch, Christopher. *The Culture of Narcissism.*
    New York: W.W. Norton & Co., Inc., 1978.

Section Two
STRATEGY

CHAPTER 4 • *Contracts*

From early in the history of man, contracts have been negotiated for business purposes. With approval, they appear in the Scriptures for marriage, and they remain useful as means to achieve social order for families and other institutions.

CHAPTER 5 • *Covenants*

Basic relationships within a culture are reflected by various kinds of covenants. Through covenant rights, institutions like business and family are formed. Covenant-making, a biblical principle practiced between man and God, is also a principle useful to human interpersonal relationships.

CHAPTER 6 • *Negotiations*

Just as businesses introduce favorable circumstances and privileges for their own personnel and customers, and as biblical precepts provide large benefit to Israel and the church, so family members maintain special and favored agreements between them.

CHAPTER 4

Contracts

● What is the purpose of business contracts?

● What is the purpose of marriage and family contracts?

> *Now this was the manner in former time in Israel concerning redeeming and concerning changing, for to confirm all things; a man plucked off his shoe, and gave it to his neighbor: and this was a testimony in Israel. Therefore the kinsman said unto Boaz, Buy it for thee. So he drew off his shoe. And Boaz said unto the elders, and unto all the people, Ye are witnesses this day, that I have bought all that was Elimelech's, and all that was Chilion's and Mahlon's, of the hand of Naomi. Moreover, Ruth the Moabitess, the wife of Mahlon, have I purchased to be my wife (Ruth 4:7-10).*

Detailed marriage contracts have been commonplace in much of the world from ancient times to the present. Marriage contracts can be traced to the earliest writings of men. They described and affirmed extensive provisions for marriage rights, dowries, personal morality and family privileges. The rights of the woman entering the marriage were sometimes stipulated or implied.

Marriage Contracts in History

The Scriptures include marriage contract negotiations. An early example is the exchange between Abraham's representative and Laban and Bethuel for the purpose of betrothing Rebekah to Isaac. When the contract arrangements were completed, Rebekah was afforded the final word of approval or disapproval. She approved (Gen. 24:57-58).

Details for the contractual agreement in the marriage of Ruth and Boaz appear in the book bearing her name (see Scripture quotation above). The arrangement was known as levirate marriage, a cultural provision highly regarded in ancient times. It was effective to care for young widows who, without children, would not be protected or cared for in old age. Ruth, a widow, returned with her mother-in-law, Naomi, to the land of Naomi's citizenship. According to Jewish tradition, the next of kin to the dead husband was expected to contract marriage with the young widow and generate a son to be reared in the name of the dead husband, Mahlon.

The next of kin passed the duty and privilege to Boaz, who contracted for Ruth and the inheritance land of Mahlon. Calling for witnesses and acknowledging the terms of the contract orally, Boaz drew off his shoe and handed it to the next of kin. This gesture was analogous to our practice of signing one's name to a piece of paper in the presence of witnesses. In that ancient time, shoes or sandals and an array of witnesses were more plentiful than writing tablets. In the place of a shoe we use a notary's seal.

Boaz and Ruth were married. Their first child, Obed, was delivered into the hands of Naomi, mother of the deceased Mahlon. The child became the heir, not of Boaz, but of Mahlon, as the levirate contract would have it. By this means—contract—a man was not without issue to bear his name.

For millennia tribes and societies designed marriages by arrangement, that is, by contract. One tradition holds that Mary and Joseph were betrothed through the offices of their synagogue. Even in modern times there are arranged marriages among some cultures and peoples. The writer of the musical, *Fiddler on the Roof,* wrote a piece entitled, "Matchmaker, matchmaker, make me a match." One of the subplots of the story relates to the progress of the nego-

tiations and the effects on the families of girl and boy
while the old matchmaker worked on an engagement
program.

Early in American history, parents of boy and girl would
meet together to design a plan for the betrothal of their
children. One set of parents would offer a few acres to the
newlyweds, the other would provide lumber or logs for a
house, and both families would help build. Even furniture
pieces might be transferred, and all matters were agreed to
before marriage. The ancient dowry system evolved into
the later tradition of a hope chest for the young bride.
Family heirlooms were passed on, often before the elders'
deaths.

While I was attending the University of Washington,
studying to earn a doctorate, a young Chinese student,
about 25 years of age, completed his graduate studies for a
master's degree. Believing it to be time for marriage, he
wrote his father in Taiwan to send him a bride. The story,
unusual by American mores, made the front page of the
Washington Daily. The choice was made in negotiations
between parents of the man and woman. The young
woman and the student were betrothed and married, even
though they were virtually strangers. When challenged
about whether or not he would love her, the young man
said, "My parents love me. Her parents love her. They
would do nothing to hurt us. I will love her, and she will
love me. Besides, when I check the divorce statistics in my
country, and those in yours, I think we have the better of
it."

History, including biblical history, is rich with precedent for marriage contracts. They were more detailed
and taken more seriously by society in former centuries
than in the twentieth. We assume that, with appropriate
sophistication, moderns might well design contracts to
meet personal needs and strengthen marriages.

Business Contracts in Society

Contractual agreements are standard for businesses.

Businesses would flounder without them. There are different types of agreements, but the basic concept is that there is a party of the first part who will take specific actions to meet the expectations of the party of the second part. Consideration, usually in the form of money, will be paid for reciprocal consideration, usually goods or services or both. An insurance policy is a contract. For a premium (an amount of money) paid, a person is provided a specific protection that is returned to him in the event of accident or death or some other circumstance.

Written contracts are necessary because circumstances change, people forget, and parties tend to interpret their interests to their own advantage. Human nature requires an orderly and verifiable means to protect people and preserve elements of equity even between family members. Contract-making is a civil way in which individuals may join in a corporate enterprise, keeping the rights of individualism but negotiating some benefits for larger ones, or preferred ones, for a mutual good.

Businesses are commonly concerned with structure, systems and strategies. Strategies relate to planning, or courses of action to utilize all available resources, within time frames, to accomplish specific goals. One aspect of planning is contractual among parties to guide activity and make matters and expectations equitable. In the college where I have current responsibility we recently requested a bid on roof repair. The bid was received, approved and a contract requested. Two items that I wished to have included were not covered at first: (1) how many years would the completed project be guaranteed, and (2) what guarantee would relate to any skylight leakage? The company returned with a written guarantee for three years on workmanship, and we agreed to close off the skylights (no longer useful), and the roofers would cover the areas with appropriate materials and provide a full guarantee. We signed the contract as amended. It was an appreciated business practice that satisfactory boundaries be determined in advance.

Marriage Contracts in Modern Life

A modern marriage license is a contract which, when its marriage has been solemnized and consummated, is treated as a perpetual legal agreement. It is so interpreted by the state. While some business contracts may be temporary to accomplish their purposes, most marriage contracts throughout history have been presumed to be lifetime agreements.

The only way a marriage contract can be ended legally is through death of its parties or by another contract called a decree of divorce. Traditionally, the divorce contract awards some indemnity to the wife and dependent children who must function without the benefits of the previous marriage contract, a contract now abrogated. Changes in tradition have been made during the latter part of the twentieth century so that husbands may also receive alimony or settlements.

The various states or provinces, following cultural tradition, provide an official contract, commonly called a license, giving legal status to marriage. In this way a marriage becomes a type of legal incorporation with rights and privileges established, by and large, through long accepted practices in the general culture. Legal or social contracts for marriage have a proved value to any society. Basic rights and privileges are generally assumed without stipulation. For example, sexual consummation of a marriage is everywhere assumed. If consummation does not follow marriage vows, the marriage may be annulled, rather than divorced, and the parties are presumed to have never married.

Beyond the legal contract is the personal one, a creative design for a particular marriage. It is the appropriate successor to family agreements of parents and has been taken over by the couple in the marriage. Personal or private contract patterns are discussed in the next chapters of this section.

In addition to officially licensed marriage contracts,

there are unofficial marriage contracts. These may be only oral, but they too are contracts—if personal promises have serious meaning. The simplest, most casual, is common-law marriage. When a man and woman live together as marrieds do, but do not follow legal procedures to marriage, they are said to be in "common-law marriage."

For standard government practice, until recent decades, continuous cohabitation of a couple was sufficient to declare them married. If oral promises were made and could be proved in court, the promises were taken as legally binding. States gradually withdrew from legalization of casual cohabitation. As the number of liaisons increased, however, so did court cases in which injured parties attempted to establish legality for the relationships, at least a legality that would compel sharing property gained during the life of the relationship. The problem remained: could alleged promises be verified by witnesses? If not, the act of living together was insufficient cause to gain legal rights for the liaison. The eminent case, establishing precedent, is the Lee Marvin trial. Sued by his live-in-girlfriend of several years, the actor Marvin won his defense in the case. He did not have to share wealth earned during the liaison. Following the case, several states have passed laws to protect both parties in cohabiting situations. After the Marvin trial, California passed a "palimony" law so that persons were given the right to sue for community property claims even if they were not legally married.

Without the legal contract or license, parties will be inconsistent to expect protection of law, or full security of rights related to traditional family experience, or approval by the general society. Those parties seem to be cavalier about law, using it to gain what they want personally (property benefits), but evading social goods (legal marriage).

Marriage Contracts Downgraded

Romantics have often criticized private marriage contracts between newlyweds, arguing that love and trust are sufficiently meaningful to maintain a marriage. They believe these agreements violate ideals which are supposed to be motivation enough for a couple. They hold that the basic license of the state is sufficient, requiring no embellishments. Love is above contract limitations. Contracts cannot harness or control love. So their argument proceeds.

Others—such as disillusioned men and women— may reject even the standard license, arguing that living together requires no agreement at all—a bizarre claim generally unworkable for a lengthy period of time in any situation between two or more persons. But even if casual liaison were acceptable to society, its rate of failure should be sufficient reason to make it unattractive even to the least discerning population.

Casual couples tend to dissolve their relationships within a matter of months. If children are born to them, those children, in too great a number, become wards of the state, or must be cared for by interested friends or relatives, or must be supported by welfare. A high number of these children become delinquent, and even when they fit into society, they often feel unhappy without family roots. Such offspring lose respect for institutions because their parents, irresponsible regarding the institution of marriage, generally possess less loyalty to other institutions like church, school or government. Those children yearn, unknowingly, for the most part, for boundaries and identity unavailable to them.

Some counselors also downgrade marriage contracts. (Others in counseling fields strongly support contracts. Whatever one believes in matters like these, he may rest assured that he can find an "authority" to prove his position.) The public receives much of what is being taught about marriage from persons who either failed at marriage themselves or who are confused about what to do with marriage failure. The late Margaret Mead, thrice-married, suggested two types of marriages: "individual" and "parental." Individual marriages for young people would legalize cohabitation for the primary purpose of friendship and sexual intimacy. No children would be generated, and no permanence would be attached to the marriage. Dissolving this marriage, the man and woman would be free to establish a mature or "parental" marriage with another mate, in which having children could be encouraged.

The Mead suggestion is patently unsatisfactory as policy. Even now—without marriage and with contraceptive precaution—youthful sexual experiences often lead to pregnancy. How would this be improved with the Mead plan? There is reason to believe the birth rate would increase if "individual" marriage were approved.

How many persons can marry only for passion and develop high ideals so that they can, without deep regret, forget the early intimacy and accept easily new marriage experiences? Would not the second mate, in the parental marriage, likely have served as a sexual playmate in a previous individual marriage? Why could not the first marriage, well planned, achieve all that either person might wish to have for life? Many other questions might be raised on the plan, questions that would increase doubt about its usefulness. However, the Mead suggestion was never taken seriously.

Other voices have been raised favoring temporary contracts. Charles Templeton, himself twice divorced, has stated: "I think marriage should be the basis of a renewable contract of three to five years." Relatively few couples, however, feel really comfortable with transient agreements for matters of such moment as marriage. They seem to feel that any belief in temporary relationships tends to assure just that—temporary rather than lasting relationships.

From the other side of the discussion, there are some theorists who would reject all contracts, arguing that such agreements do not make marriages stronger. Even Carl Rogers, the eminent psychologist, criticizes contract styles. Amitai Etzioni, highly respected Columbia University professor and writer, argues against contracts in marriage, emphasizing the possibility that contracts reduce the solidarity and integrity of marriage. He objects to the comparison of marriage with business implied by use of contracts. The differences, he feels, are too great. Longevity for marriage, he would argue, is a significant feature separating its nature from that of business agreements. Etzioni wants in marriage much of what we would defend here for family solidarity. If the problems cited by Etzioni were necessary, a defense of contracts would not be attempted here. Contracts, like life insurance, or retirement programs, are written for life, or can be. If they are, they are presumed to be superior contracts for their purpose. Even persons who do not complete long life marriages commonly admit that an effective lifetime family is an ideal, superior to any other, but for them the imperfections of mankind make long term seem impracticable. It might well be that careful review of contractual matters would bring marriage and family problems to the early attention of parties. In this way some later incidents in experience and learnings might be avoided. More marriages would survive.

The assumption in this writing is that contracts can make an unbroken marriage a happier one, easier to manage, and stronger. The very existence of agreements is tacit knowledge that, even in a love relationship, human weakness and foibles can be treated, reducing hurts between persons. The contracts are between persons to protect the institution. The institution fails only when the persons in it fail.

Just as contracts for employment, for building structures, for purchase of land differ from one another because of their intrinsic and social differences, so marriage contracts also have their special meanings. Like any analogy, the one between marriage and general business is incomplete, not holding up in every detail. Yet a review of the best features of business contracts suggests principles in family practice that can improve marriage.

Features in Contracts

A marriage license, as noted earlier, is a contract. In many states and provinces, the granting of the contract privilege to applicants requires proof of good health (at least as perceived through blood testing), that the applicants are not near relatives (at least not above second cousins on the family tree), and that they are socially approved (at least they are identifiable as citizens, or approved through a waiting period, or some other means of recognition).

This contract assumes conjugal rights for the parties, and provides certain immunities such as any requirement to testify in court against each other. Although society has reduced somewhat the financial responsibilities of mates for each other, there remains large duty for the debts of both, as well as privilege for mutual accumulations of wealth. In the absence of any other contract, like a will, mates are presumed to be the heirs of each other.

Whatever additional legal contract may be drawn between marriage parties, it must be appropriate to the laws of the land. For example, a contract would not stand up in court if it denied the rights of children born to the couple. A man, not wishing to have children and contracting with his wife to evade children, could not legally sign away responsibility to a child if he fathered the infant. The mother could not reject alimony to care for her child by this husband, unless she could show that she had adequate income through her own employment, or some other source.

Some contracts are related to agreements such as behavioral contracts designed to change conduct on one or more habits. They introduce order, cut down on abrasive conflicts, improve communications, make the problem, not the person, the enemy to be conquered. These agreements are made, accomplish change, and sometimes are quickly forgotten.

One of the most poignant covenant-contracts I have

ever read was designed by a couple during a difficult period of their marriage. The wife was a young Christian who had set aside her former habits and attitudes two or three years prior to the contract writing. Her husband, a rising junior executive, was not a Christian. He was negative and cynical about his wife's experience and the activities she followed as a devout person. She was a teacher, and he worked in a downtown office twenty or thirty miles distant from home. At length they discussed their differences and concerns, stating them in contract form. The following composition was agreed on:

A—THE WIFE	B—THE HUSBAND
1. A will prepare a light breakfast for B for the mornings.	B will eat breakfast.
2. A will complete housework before B comes home so he won't feel she just got in.	B will take train home regularly.
3. A will prepare light dinner for B.	B will not drink cocktails and fill up on hors d'oeuvres before coming home; if B wants big dinner he will let A know in advance.
4. A will discourage students from calling her when B is home.	B will be tolerant of emergency situations.

5. A will serve dinner in kitchen or dining room.

   B will not watch TV or read newspaper during dinner, but communicate with A.

6. After dinner, A will be tolerant of B's TV programs.

   B will be tolerant of A's TV or radio requests.

7. A will not object to B's reading material.

   B will not make fun of A's reading material.

8. A is not a nun and is ready for intimacy at any time.

   B will not reject A's physical advances or expressions of affection.

9. A will happily participate in daily exercise or sports with B.

   B will discipline himself to exercise or play a sport daily to get in good physical shape.

10. A does not wish to drink alcoholic beverages.

    B will not force A to drink or make fun of her when she doesn't.

11. A will attend church and leave B alone only once a week.

    B will not make fun of A for attending church or make her feel guilty for leaving him.

12. A enjoys meeting B's friends and socializing with them.

    B should not object to meeting A's friends and socializing with them.

13.	A will be flexible about when she attends church and will accompany B on weekend trips.	B will plan weekend trips and activities for A and B to do together.
14.	A will continue teaching . . . coping with the Establishment.	B will continue his private studying . . . and will practice speaking with A.
15.	A will communicate honestly with B when problems arise.	B will communicate honestly with A when problems arise.
16.	A loves B and wants to stay married to him always.	B loves A and should try to work out problems so that he will want to continue his marriage with A.

Several years following the mutual agreement, the husband became a Christian, and together he and his wife began to build a Christian marriage. The contract held the two of them together, at least until their shared Christian commitment could help them solve problems. They succeeded admirably.

The contracts referred to in this writing are not all legally binding. Most are related to the covenant of marriage, a spiritual and invisible force that is vital to marriage solidarity, especially for Christian marriage. The Scriptures include this covenant perception in passages like Ephesians, chapter 5, and by implication in many other references.

During recent years there has been a renewed interest in

the concept of passages in individual lives and for families.
The renewal of interest arose from Erik Erikson's research,
so widely publicized in Gail Sheely's book, *Passages*.
Whitehead and Whitehead added their perceptions to the
discussion when they pointed out that "passage" for persons is much more than surviving a confusing time in life.
The passage, well managed, is life-changing and beneficial.
It may mean separation from something, then working
through a marginal period in life that is transitional to the
reintegration phase of the whole experience. Israel's exit
from Egypt, followed by the wilderness experience and the
arrival into the promised land, is a magnificent metaphor
of the process.

One of the great issues is to learn to let go of what precedes the new. Letting go is sometimes helped when the
person or couple learns negotiation and contract making.

Reading Related to Contracts

Authors with Christian or generally Christian emphases:

Collins, Gary R. (Editor). *Make More of Your Marriage.* Waco, Tex.: Word Books. (pp. 122-133, "A Model for Marital Therapy," Donald F. Tweedie, Jr. [Note Bibliography.])

Whitehead, Evelyn Eaton and James D. *Marrying Well.* Garden City, N.Y.: Doubleday & Co., Inc., 1981. (p. 61 ff.)

Wright, H. Norman. *Premarital Counseling.* Chicago: Moody Press, 1977.

CHAPTER 5

Covenants

- **What is a covenant of good will for business?**

- **What is a covenant of love in a marriage?**

> *For this cause shall a man leave his father and mother, and shall be joined unto his wife, and they two shall be one flesh. This is a great mystery: but I speak concerning Christ and the church (Eph. 5:31-32).*

> *. . . for the marriage of the Lamb is come, and his wife hath made herself ready. . . . And the Spirit and the bride say, Come . . . (Rev. 19:7; 22:17).*

As they are commonly understood in society, most contracts are presumed to hold legal standing. They follow rigid laws and because of some technicality can easily be declared invalid. They are perceived as constructed in equal parts so that the benefits guaranteed to one party are presumed to equate with benefits accruing to the second party. But there is a higher contract and exchange system in operation among human beings. In this is covenant making. We rightly elevate it above contractual agreements as those agreements are generally perceived. A covenant has spiritual force.

As noted above, a properly executed contract may have legal force. It is an agreement between two parties, each party protecting his own benefit. It has to do with material, time, action, and service. A marriage contract or license is like this in that it has legal force and is based on a social or business agreement. A covenant is larger and not easily stated in common equations that are perceived by all persons in the same way. A covenant requires the response of the human will and spirit. It implies a close, deep relationship between two or more parties, for the benefit of the relationship, not solely for the benefit of each separately. Usually it is not perceived as a competitive or confrontational experience. The will of each party is partly yielded to the will of the other to insure that the relationship remains lasting and meaningful.

The play of understanding between contract and covenant is partly addressed by Whitehead and Whitehead in their fine volume, *Marrying Well.* They write:

In the Middle East during the first millennium before the time of Christ, the notion of covenant embraced a variety of pacts and agreements—from trade agreements between clans and nations to marriage pacts between families. A covenant, then, was a reciprocally binding agreement between parties (Whitehead & Whitehead 1981, 63).

But the idea of covenant, write Whitehead and Whitehead, took on a subtle nuance as Israel began to use the idea as expressive of its tribal relationship to God. Covenant, in this sense, became unconditional, therefore lasting. It became more than a contract or business transaction. Marriage began to gain this covenant position of total life commitment.

It is possible, of course, to reduce marriage to contract, without covenant. But we nowhere defend that practice. Contract must be made in marriage only under covenant commitments. Whitehead and Whitehead, writing as lay Catholic authors, point out that part of reform in the Roman Catholic church, through the Second Vatican Council, "has been the return to the imagery of covenant in understanding Christian marriage" (Whitehead & Whitehead 1981, 65).

Spiritual Covenants

The biblical account includes many covenants, principally between man and God. God maintained a covenant relationship with Adam and Eve during the Eden experience. On betrayal of their part in the covenant, Adam and Eve were given another relating to labor, childbearing, and a hostile environment. Later, Noah received the covenant of the rainbow, a guarantee that the world would not be destroyed again by water. Even later, Moses and Israel received the covenant of redemption, continued in the covenant of perpetuity for the line of King David.

When Israel would no longer maintain covenant commitments to God, there was mutual withdrawal at distances determined by the degree of the various separations between the parties. Jeremiah used the analogy of marriage early in his prophetic writings (chap. 3) and deplored the violation by Israel until the covenant had to be ended: *I had put her away, and given her a bill of divorce* (3:8). Jeremiah, throughout the chapter, reminded the people of their marriage and the ultimate achievement of the covenant promise. When the fulfillment would come, they would no longer need the remembrance of the Ark of the Covenant. What was covenant would be completed in experience if the people would follow their commitment to relationship.

Certainly the new covenant presented in Hebrews 8 is the most important of all covenants, describing the redemptive meaning of Christ. It is compared, or contrasted, with the older covenant to Israel, and the new is made superior. One gains the impression from Scripture that a covenant in one instance may be satisfactory and complete, but another may be larger and better. The meaning here is growth. The greater the wisdom, the maturity, the love perception, the higher will be the covenant, and the more satisfying the experience within the covenant. The covenant of ultimate spiritual marriage between Christ and the Church is proclaimed by the Apostle Paul to be a mystery

(Eph. 5:32). Perhaps in that mystery the covenant of marriage between a man and woman may be sealed for their lifetimes.

For centuries devout men and women designed covenants with God. Some were cast in near contract forms. Those covenants often included statements of the writer's religious beliefs, and a list of particulars. Here the writer would promise fealty to God, and would either reject any wish to change his covenant, or would provide the only means for amending it. Some means for strengthening his resolve might be entered in the belief the covenant would grow. From time to time, perhaps on an annual basis, the covenant was reviewed to determine if it was being kept.

Of the many stories about covenants, the one about Albert Benjamin Simpson told by A.W. Tozer, is poignant:

> At seventeen he decides—as a result of reading again his father's old favorite, Dodridge—to confirm his spiritual experience by a solemn covenant with God, as the party of the first part, and himself, as the party of the second part, being the high contracting parties. . . . He set aside a whole day for fasting and prayer, and then at the close of the day draws up and signs and seals the covenant.

> This covenant is one of the most remarkable things produced by any boy-Christian in any period of the Church's history. . . . The covenant itself runs into about nine-hundred words (Tozer 1943, 22-28).

Tozer reviewed the covenant (actually a mixture of covenant and contract), beginning with its prayer, followed by statements about God's holiness and man's depravity, especially Simpson's own. He affirmed his faith and ended with a benediction:

> Now give me Thy Spirit and Thy protection in my heart at all times, and then I shall drink of the rivers of

salvation, lie down by still waters, and be infinitely happy in the favor of God (Tozer 1943, 28).

Once this matter was settled, Tozer wrote, ". . . this mighty purpose took over and drove him like a benignant master for the rest of his days" (Tozer 1943, 29).

The argument we would make here is that marriage is more to be understood in its covenant relationship than in its contractual. The license to marry is the ticket presented at the gate of a larger life. Once admission is gained, we tend to fall back on the life of covenant relationship found in fidelity, trust, love, peace, growth. None of these can be reduced to contract, but all are enhanced by covenant commitment. The covenant is designed for the whole of life.

Covenant Meanings in Business

Society provides many examples of business and social covenants. The Constitution of the United States is a covenant between the citizens and the government. It describes rights, responsibilities and privileges of the parties in order to secure a long-lasting relationship that is workable and desirable. From this covenant many smaller ones, like state constitutions, emerge. In an attempt to make the covenants workable in an expanding society, laws are passed. Laws link contracts to covenants.

A birth certificate is evidence of the covenant of citizenship. A passport is also evidence of the covenant of citizenship in the country issuing that document to any person. A driver's license is evidence of a citizen's privilege. Without it the individual may not drive legally. If he does drive without license, he violates at least one of the meanings of liberty; namely, protection of the rights of others.

Business life, as we would have it understood, is dependent on a belief in the best that man can become. When that perception is lost or abandoned, business sinks. It loses its covenant meaning and translates business meaning into self-aggrandizement, greed, materialism and distorted

competition. It is about this decline that Richard Pascale
and Anthony Athos feel compelled to address the business
world about the quality of the finest business houses. As
we review their ideas elsewhere in this writing, Pascale
and Athos relate that quality to family and value (sometimes religious value) systems.

Harry Levinson, cited earlier, is summarized by Daniel
Goleman on this issue of covenant meaning, which he
names "psychological contract":

> Levinson contends that workers and management estab-
> lish, along with wage contracts, a set of tacit "psycho-
> logical contracts" that govern how they will act toward
> each other. Much on-the-job unhappiness, he thinks, is
> due to the violation of these implicit contracts (Gole-
> man 1977, 45).

Marriage Covenants

If the highest of all relationships, that of a believer with
God, may be strengthened and deepened by a covenant,
why should not husband and wife enhance their relationship with a covenant between them? The first step is to
discuss the covenant concept itself until both parties feel
comfortable in accepting ideas pertaining to intimate commitments directed toward specific ends in the marriage relationship.

The covenant concept in marriage is accented in the
wedding band, an emblem of the eternal God—no beginning and no end. An exchange of rings in a ceremony
implies the covenant of marriage based on the integrity of
God's being. The spiritual character of a marriage contract is kept in evidence by the unbroken circle. Traditionally, the ring has been plain, rather than ornate, so basic
clarity in the concept might be maintained without dis-
traction. It is believed to need no embellishment.

Traditional marriage ceremonies state or imply covenant
meaning in the family. Marriage is a "holy estate" founded
by God "in the time of man's innocency." Covenant based

on divine acts is significant enough to replace biology as primary commitment in human relationship. Parents (biological) lose primacy to the mates (covenant) of their children. To "love, honor and obey" is to enter covenant relationship. Unlike the specific features of a contract, factors of a covenant relationship are difficult to measure. They shift, undulate, change. The marriage will either grow or weaken, and that unevenly.

Marriages inevitably change as the persons in them change. Those marriages may be left alone to shift as forces, sometimes invisible, move them. Or the parties may take the reins of their lives and direct their family destinies. Establishing a covenant relationship helps them to hold together through the various phases of change.

Large Phases in Marriage

Some analysts cast marriages into three large phases. The first is the *passion and games* phase. Marriage is perceived as a legitimate context for the expression of sexual appetites. Free of guilt, the couple begins to experiment with serious intimacy. Often the period is marked by playing out various games, sometimes gracefully and sometimes competitively, as the wife and husband wrestle with their identity together and as individuals. These two purposes, corporate and individual, often collide to create tension.

At this writing I am counseling a young woman who is trying to sift out the passion and games phase of her marriage. Not marrying until her late twenties, she brought a mature single life pattern to her new relationship. She could have lived out her life alone without frustration. She was in full control of her passions, was occupied in superior employment, was culturally progressed so as to fill her life with literature, art and appropriate social interests.

She chose to marry. But her marriage reduced more significantly than she thought it would the "alone" time she enjoyed. On occasion she does not wish to be touched, to be involved with another, to be responsible for this or

that duty. Her husband interprets her wishes as evidence
of coldness, perhaps flagging love. Although the marriage
is only six months old, the parties will require more coun-
selling if the marriage is to hold together and they are to
find happiness. The first phase of the husband/wife experience quickly became insufficient. They came early to the
second phase. A contract allowing the private time, differentials in interests, and other matters would greatly assist
the marriage. A third party will be useful in drafting it.

The second phase is the *tension and conflict* period,
when first differences between partners ripen. Each
member thrusts and retreats, talks and falls silent, takes
blame and ascribes it to the other at the same time. If the
spiral circles downward, the marriage is likely doomed. If
the parties are alert, they will perceive what is happening
and take steps to change things, to understand, to adjust
and to accept some differentials. They will focus on advantages rather than disadvantages.

Phase three is the happiest, the most comfortable stage.
Maturity and acceptance characterize the period. It is a
marriage of accord. Husband and wife feel happy with
each other. They prefer the company of each other over
anyone else. They adapt and discover that each is somehow like the other. Either tends to do what the other does.
Expectations are no longer forced, but are amended to fit
circumstances. Irritations, contradictions, habits are cast
into perspective. They are no longer threatening either to
personal peace or to solidarity in the covenant relationship
itself.

The first two phases may be more easily weathered and
transitions will be smoother if agreements are worked out,
sometimes hammered out, for the benefit of the individual
family. Key to the process is a sensitive attitude and
willingness to utilize planning programs to solve problems
or to blunt the edge of potential problems. If this system is
perceived as too mechanical, lacking in trust and generosity, or too hard work, it will not likely be adopted. If it
is accepted as a practical means for developing ideals,

expressing mutual faith and personal commitment, the effort will be well rewarded.

Covenant-Contracts

Whitehead and Whitehead cast our case well when they wrote:

> These two powerful images of marriage—as covenant and as contract—are part of our religious heritage. These are not mutually exclusive notions: both are binding commitments between parties which include reciprocal rights and obligations. . . . With this covenant we commit ourselves to each other unconditionally. . . . But we also need to continue to clarify our own expectations and hopes for this relationship: a contractlike specifying of these expectations may well assist this covenant to grow and endure (Whitehead and Whitehead 1981, 66).

Unlike the Protestant tradition, the Catholic view of Whitehead and Whitehead would carry this covenant perception to the point of making marriage, for Catholics, a sacrament. It is apparent that for Catholics marriage will remain a sacrament, and for Protestants it is not and will not be a sacrament. But for both the covenant perception remains as ancient and biblical.

Marriage covenants presume moral and ethical foundations. When covenants have been drawn and the marriage members feel gratified that high principles will prevail, the family gets on with the business of living. Many couples seldom return to their covenant statements after a satisfactory pattern for living emerges for them. Having elevated the awareness of their concerns, husband and wife, and later the children, function easily at a somewhat higher level than would have been the case otherwise.

Donald F. Tweedie, Jr. adopted what he calls "Covenant Therapy." At first he thought that the word *covenant* was a synonym for *contract*. In his studies he discovered the

meaningful differential between the two words. There are
discriminating differences, with covenant therapy a more
"Godlike," gracious and personal procedure. All divine and
human relationships "may be expressed as facets of a
covenant." Most covenants are "implicit and covert." Contracts are "explicit and overt." Covenants change somewhat during the passage of time. These changes show in
covenant modifications. When relationships are improved,
there is covenanted renewal. Tweedie reviewed a covenant
therapy case and completed his discussion by affirming
that such therapy is "based upon a radically biblical model
of man" (Tweedie 1976, 130-32).

The keeping of the covenant must depend on the
integrity of the makers—integrity based on love, empathy,
intimacy and motivation. If those virtues are absent the
agreements tend to dissolve. Seldom are they introduced
into a court of law for adjudication. Their force is in the
quality of the married persons. An example is the agreement between my wife and me that we would never use
divorce as a means for problem solving. Such an agreement
would have no legal force, but it had great force for us.

Many couples make promises or design procedures
which read like personal contracts to reinforce their covenants. My wife and I made several consensus statements
early in our marriage that were implemented in our later
experiences with each other. One of these was that if we
should come to impasse on anything "inside the house," her
opinion would prevail. Mine would hold on unresolved
issues "outside the house." If I wished to have a couch
located on the east side of the room and she wished to
have it on the west, it would be placed west. (I might not
sit on it, but it would go west.) If we should disagree on
the make or color of automobile to be purchased, I would
have my way. In more than forty years of marriage
the agreement may have been invoked four or five times.
Neither of us recalls a number. We know that the
agreement, made in good humor, works very well. It was
an available thing—if needed. Its greatest use was to make

each of us feel sufficiently flexible about issues. Knowing it was there was really all we needed of it.

Christian couples sometimes prepare covenant-contracts as means for affirming their ideals. Such a contract was forged in 1961 by a man and woman on the eve of their marriage. In partial summary, it read as follows:

1. Authority: He is the head of the house, etc. . . .
2. Division of Labor: Essentially, he provides the money, she does household chores, although he does outside work and repairs. . . .
3. Children: Agree on four. . . .
4. Money: Budget, and he is in charge of bill paying. . . .
5. Sex: There will be no extramarital sexual activity. . . .
6. Religion: We will support the same church with attendance, money and service. . . .
We will take the children to church. . . .
7. Personal Privacy: Each has a right to privacy and his own ideas without scorn. . . .
Neither will open the other's mail. . . .
Social engagements are to be made after consultation. . . .
8. Miscellaneous: Differences in art tastes mean we will make alternate selections. . . .
Each will live according to standards of Christian morality and citizenship.

One of the articles in the original contract referred to above was related to the differences in the artistic tastes of the husband and wife. Each last day of the month was time for taking down the paintings in the house and hanging others in their place. On alternate months the husband's choices were hung, and removed for her choices at the end of the next month. We might reject the ritual as troublesome, but why not make the changes systematically? One imagines that the agreement made the home more exciting, and created interesting conversation. It probably provided a better means for problem solving than many friends of the couple had found.

A personal covenant in a marriage is useful because it can relate practically to the need of persons for order, which is social; for well-being, which is physical; for meaning, which is intellectual; and for values, which are spiritual. The covenant concept appears to respect both individual and corporate values in a marriage.

Reading about Contracts and the Family

Authors with Christian or generally Christian emphases:

Collins, Gary R. *Make More of Your Marriage.* Waco, Texas: Word Books, 1976. (Chap. 9, pp. 122-33.)

Hickey, Marilyn. *God's Covenant for Your Family.* Tulsa, Okla.: Harrison House, 1977.

Whitehead, Evelyn Eaton and James D. *Marrying Well.* Garden City, New York: Doubleday & Co., Inc., 1981. (p. 63 ff.) (Catholic context.)

CHAPTER 6

Negotiations

- **How do negotiations focus on business contracts?**

- **How may marriage purposes be guided by negotiations?**

> *They put it [the money] in the hand of the workmen that had oversight of the house of the Lord, and they gave it to the workmen that wrought in the house of the Lord, to repair and amend the house (2 Chron. 34:10).*

Agreements between individuals or corporate entities do not spring instantly into being. In order to reach acceptable decisions, people often engage in some sort of bargaining or system of exchange between themselves. In these negotiations and systems, the advantages for both sides must be perceived as essentially equal in value.

Negotiations in the Scriptures

The Bible implies approval of negotiations as a legitimate way to solve problems, both personal and interpersonal. In patriarchal times fathers, if they did not directly act themselves, would send forth trusted servants to negotiate marriages for their children. Such a servant was sent by Abraham to negotiate a betrothal agreement for Rebekah to Isaac. Samson requested his parents to negotiate for his wife. Others, like Jacob and Boaz, in the absence of family representatives, carried on their own negotiations. Some arrangements, as those of King Saul for his daughters, were less idealistic than even those living at the time would have hoped for. Saul's promise to give his daughters in exchange for a soldier's success in battle repels us. The offer was not immediately taken by David, who preferred to pass over Saul's first daughter to win the second, Michal. Saul's devious ways were used, in part, by David to gain the woman of his choice.

Even more objectionable than Saul's opportunism was Lot's negotiations to give up his daughters for participation with the sordid crowd in order to avoid any violation of his guests. But we do not reject an excellent technique because it may be used in wrong ways, for wrong purposes. We admire the negotiations of Abraham for a burial cave for his wife, of Moses with Hobab and Jethro, of David with Abigail, of Boaz with Naomi and Ruth, of Joseph with Pharaoh in Egypt, and Hosea for his wife.

In the New Testament numerous instances of negotiation occur. The infant church in the book of Acts of the Apostles negotiate through the transition from law to grace, from Jewry to the holy church, made up of all peoples, and from exclusiveness in the Old Testament to the whole Scripture. Jesus taught His disciples how to negotiate for the purposes of the gospel. If they were rejected, He would have them shake off shoe dust as witness against intransigent peoples in the towns they visited.

If the issue is moral and clear, no negotiation is appropriate for the Christian, if the negotiation violates his morality. In such a case, where no legitimate compromise exists, he pays the price of his convictions. Jesus refused to negotiate with Herod or Pilate to save His life. Undaunted, Pilate would negotiate Jesus' release but was resisted by religious leaders, not so much from moral conviction as from self-interest, pride and intransigency. The point to be made here is that negotiations provide a civil way to solve problems among imperfect men. Because virtue and weakness are present in all persons, negotiation becomes legitimate in search of the best of imperfect solutions. When there is a divine commandment to guide us, we suspend negotiations about the matter. Because a perfect voice has spoken, there is no need to look for alternatives.

The issues are sometimes mixed between matters decided and matters to be decided. For example, Christian marriage is well defined (Eph. 5:21-33). There is no justification for diluting that meaning. It is not open for change. However, to negotiate approval of this woman to be married to this man in a clearly ordered Christian marriage is appropriate. The Apostle Paul provides some guidance in this negotiating process (1 Cor. 7). In our time the negotiations are largely in the hands of the man and woman to be married. But the principles remain.

Negotiations for Business

Governments and businesses hold some notions about where they are going, what they wish to do, and how they expect to function. When these direction finders are too vague, both representatives of the institutions and the people with whom they deal feel confused and uncertain about related matters, and sometimes about themselves. A prime illustration of failure on the part of the United States occurred in the United Nations early in June, 1982. On a vote relative to the Falkland crisis between Great Britain and Argentina, the American ambassador, Jeane Kirkpatrick, sided with Britain. In a matter of minutes, and following announcement of the vote, the ambassador announced that if the vote were eligible for change she would be instructed by her government to abstain. On the television news that evening Americans were, with Ambassador Kirkpatrick, embarrassed at the clumsiness of their government's approach.

In a speech a day or so later, Ambassador Kirkpatrick, perhaps smarting from her embarrassment, stated that the United States is "impotent" in the United Nations because "we simply have behaved like a bunch of amateurs." She reflected on "our unhappy fall from influence to impotence." Among our problems, she said, is an inability to express a cohesive national purpose. Instead we stumble "from issue to issue" (Denver Post, June 8, 1982, p. 3A).

When a nation, business or family has no clear definitions of itself, its purpose, its non-negotiables, its perception of others, it will not do well in working out problems to effective solutions.

When negotiations are carried through in an environment where there is mutual understanding of the human condition (virtue and weakness) there is reason to hope for success. Out of negotiations written agreements are developed to launch programs, to settle differences, to assign responsibilities, and to stipulate details. In this way ideals and expectations are formulated in practical terms. Such agreements keep the parties on track to their ultimate purposes.

Agreements between nations are sometimes called treaties. History is strewn with broken treaties, but the absence of any treaties at all would have left the world in greater chaos than we or our forefathers have experienced. Most treaties have been kept sufficiently well that friendly nations continue treaty making with general success.

Negotiations occur, or should occur, when the wishes, rights, or privileges of parties in some relationship to each other might come into conflict. Human depravity guarantees human conflict. Mature persons wish to defuse conflict. To solve the problems we ought to learn the art of negotiation, which is trade-off. One gives up some things so he may get others. His friendly opposite also yields for his gains. Negotiations are carried on most effectively in a noncompetitive atmosphere. There are no winners and losers in the usual meanings of those words.

Negotiating in business is often carried on in a competitive manner. Adversarial roles are taken between management and labor. Confrontation, harsh language and positions are struck so that fair and honorable exchange becomes difficult, if not impossible. From this adversarial position an attitude has grown in society that negotiations are one-sided so that the strong, the opinionated, even the mean, are "winners." Some books on the art of negotiation for businesses, for persons, even for family, may distort the ideals of negotiations defended here. Labor and management at each other's throats do not provide our models. Here, too, we acknowledge that collective bargaining, when properly carried through in a respectful atmosphere, is an excellent way to resolve problems in business.

Negotiating in the best sense, a negotiator requests all parties to consider their claims, weigh them, review the costs, consequences, time frames and values. Responsibilities and roles may be determined, perhaps benefits cited. Out of the exchanges, contracts, covenants or statements are concluded to assist the various parties to practice maturity in their conduct.

Negotiations for Families

Through friendly debate a couple clarifies expectations and forces them into manageable performance for their marriage. Even without any other purpose than clarification of expectations negotiations would be justified. Expectations are thus equalized or balanced. Perhaps from mutual exchange decisions can be made on everything including heirs, lifestyle, behavior including professional activity, spending, even sexual expression. Through negotiation fair and equitable contracts are drawn.

Property and Heirs

Older men and women, or propertied persons entering marriage, may contract to protect their heirs or to carry out long-held purposes. These persons may have been, and probably were, married previously and they have prospective heirs. Either through death or divorce these elders are single and plan to remarry. They often cast their wishes in contract form so they will not be misunderstood, either for their present motivations for marriage or for the distribution of their property in the event of death for either or both persons. The distribution of real property and such matters as tax considerations are studied to determine what agreements ought to be concluded. Monumental problems have arisen when written contracts were not designed to treat all family members with justice.

One of the most unusual marriage contracts of the century, in the western world, was that negotiated between Aristotle Onassis and Jacqueline Bouvier Kennedy. It reputedly covered 170 sections or paragraphs, resolving every issue either party could presume. It is reported that it stipulated sex issues, monetary guarantees for all living children, residence preferences, and other matters. On the death of Onassis, his widow and surviving daughter from an earlier marriage resolved property considerations through the articles of the marriage contract. Neither woman took the contract to court.

Lifestyle

Young couples may use contract agreements to express equality concepts. Often statements of personal preference are agreed to in writing. In this way whatever is current in social debate may actually show up in a contract. For example, with the rising interest in ecology during the last quarter of the twentieth century, some young couples have stipulated a lifestyle that would be simple, unlike that of their parents. Sexual equality statements and maintaining her maiden name were sometimes stipulated. Vocations, children, chores, and several score other topics have been included in lifestyle agreements.

Persons in professional vocations—particularly those in the public eye—may develop unusual lifestyle agreements. Married and divorced, Elizabeth Bloomer and her new husband prepared in 1948 a contract that included the number of children they would have, the principle of 75/25 give-and-take ratio between them, and the promise that neither would try to change the other. These negotiations, in all likelihood, saved the marriage—a marriage beset by problems introduced by the professional life of a politician, her husband, Gerald Ford, who later became President of the United States.

Behavior Patterns

To avoid marital difficulties husband and wife may have to design and record specific behavior they will follow. For example, a wife does well her share of work and carries responsibility for some of the earning power in the home. She does not mind cooking nearly all of the meals, even doing the dishes. But she loathes carrying out the garbage. Her husband seldom agrees to do the task himself. Actually, he agrees that his wife's request is justified and that he should respond favorably. For some reason he seldom does that to which he agrees and, in his best moments, that which he believes he ought to do. The problem might be solved with a behavioral contract.

A behavioral agreement develops trade-offs. If one thing (onerous) happens, then another (desirable) will also happen. If the first does not, then the second does not. The agreement does not become a legal matter. A behavioral contract, as noted earlier, would not be taken to court to force compliance. For example, the husband in the above story thoroughly enjoys his Saturday golf game with his friends. The behavioral contract concluded between husband and wife might incorporate this trade-off: no garbage disposal, no golf. Garbage emptied during the week means golf on Saturday. It is an old principle of discipline—denial of a pleasant experience for failure to carry through a duty.

Behavioral contracts tend to dissolve without fanfare. Once the new habit or acknowledgement has been established, the parties are gratified. There is no reason to press a contract further. The whole arrangement is construed on the good will and integrity of the parties. In six months or so the man carries out the garbage without much awareness of what he is doing. He discovers that he is not so mistreated as he at first thought he would be. That which was negotiated has become acceptable habit.

Romance and Sex

Agreements may be cast romantically. A couple may

develop statements, sometimes in poetic language, that later remind them of their earlier attitudes and help them recall how they felt at the beginning. Rather than becoming antiromantic, as sometimes alleged, such a contract can preserve romance by affirming emotions, activities (like date nights and vacations), communication (like specified gestures and words), and the like. One couple contracted to touch each other and express their love as early as convenient for them each day. Another couple agreed (wrongly, I believe) never to leave the physical sight of the other. Such an agreement takes too great advantage of contractual techniques. It asks too much of human conduct.

We have suggested that some issues are non-negotiable. The types of contracts that set aside such traditional values as sexual fidelity to mates have not, on statistical averages, worked well. Open marriage contracts have not served parties as they seemed to promise. Nena O'Neill, co-author of *Open Marriage*, the book published in 1972 that popularized agreements between mates to have other sexual liaisons, contended five years later that her research showed that fidelity is important to happiness in marriage.

Reconciliation

Negotiated contracts provide excellent technique to gain reconciliation for a couple. At odds with each other, husband and wife hurl accusations back and forth. Even in counseling, the situation worsens as recital of aggravations reinforce pervasive feelings of unfairness and injustice. The counselor ascertains which of the two, husband or wife, is stronger, especially in spiritual maturity. In private conversation with that one, he gains admission of an awareness of that strength. Further, the counselor reviews the concept of the New Testament, that the strong yield their own preferences to the weak. Part of being weak is the inflexibility and self-concern of the weak person.

Persuaded, the stronger person is prepared to make con-

cessions. The counselor extracts agreements from that one
when the weaker mate appears unable or sternly unwilling
to make adjustment. Even so, the weaker person generally
desires to give genuine cooperation. He or she begins to
feel there is no reason to fear domination or one-sided
sacrifices.

By small beginnings an agreement is developed. Skill-
fully composed, simple trade-offs are agreed to, and success is virtually assured. This early success is important to
get the couple to remain with the venture. More complex
problems are resolved later, using the same pattern. Gradually, and sometimes dramatically, the marriage is healed.

Marriage and Family Courses

Theoretical agreements may be used to prepare for marriage. College, even high school, courses in marriage and
the family often use contract systems to teach principles
and applications of those principles in life situations. Po-
tentially tense situations are created in the laboratory.
Rather than trying to fight out competing viewpoints and
finding them unresolved, students learn how to give and
take, to trade off duties and privileges, to recognize that
differences will always be present and are not evidences of
broken relationships.

Teachers in schools are generally more concerned with
process than with the resulting contracts. The large purpose of courses using contracts is to teach the art of negotiation in intimate relationships. Negotiation means understanding how the other person is thinking, then giving
some, taking some, adjusting for emergencies, balancing
privileges and duties, and feeling that every person's viewpoint, including one's own, counts for something. Each
party influences the outcome.

Family Business Contracts

Some marriage agreements are sufficiently detailed that
they include partnership contracts for business dealings,
how a family business is to be managed, how funds are to

be governed, and the like.

Numerous couples have sought counseling because of changes in their marriages created by family businesses. The scenario is a common one. Husband and wife enter into their own business. Both sacrifice themselves and, sometimes, their marriage to build the business. They are held together and are reasonably happy as long as they believe that their future will be easier and prosperous. On the doorstep of success and security one of the family members, usually the husband, may begin a studied withdrawal from the marriage. He may have found another woman. The husband, in his own apartment by this time, financially maintains his wife and family. The wife generally loses or gives up her part of the control of the business. Most family businesses are constructed around the skills and talents of the husband. The wife often performs the vital functions of the office and organization. Her part is more easily replaced than his.

A contract negotiated early in the marriage and business partnership might have served as a protective device, if not to save the marriage, at least to prevent shabby and unfair treatment of one partner by the other.

Sibling Contracts

Sibling negotiations are excellent means for solving knotty problems with children. Operating on the premise that persons, children included, are basically reasonable, a contract provides a focus for the meeting of minds. Parents, distraught with their children's conduct, might well discuss the need for order in a household, the equity of sharing chores, the rationale for parental expectations, and the like. They would listen to complaints and insights presented by their children. Together, parents and children hammer out an agreement, including sanctions (behavioral performance, rewards and penalties). Once forged, the agreement holds until amendment is accepted by all parties concerned. By this means such matters as simple household chores no longer serve as cause for sibling battles or parental frustration. In following the process, everyone is learning the art of negotiation.

This process worked well for my wife and me in child rearing. With our children, we reviewed our ideals and with them organized our conduct. They agreed to certain chores that we shifted from week to week. They worked out with us their study hours, television viewing time, and family events, including vacation spots. We had advance agreements on church attendance and home devotional times, even the agendas for them—who would read, pray, ask or answer questions. In turn the children were trusted, were rewarded, were granted privileges, were given voices and sometimes votes in family decision making. We even negotiated an agreement that no one would make a judgment about any other family member or action without first asking one or more nonjudgmental questions about the matter. The method proved ideal for us during the years of our children's dependency.

The fear that negotiations between husbands and wives or parents and children are too cold, too mechanical, is unfounded. Husband and wife, loving one another, find little problem in guaranteeing the security of both. They do not fear contracts and may feel that carefully wrought agreements provide checkpoints on the sensitive features of their marriage.

Those couples who have lost love, trust and respect in their marriages might recover by agreeing to some fairness in exchanges. The idea is worth a try; there is nothing more to lose. Families beset by sibling rivalry and bickering might well find that a contract brings peace to the household. In the development of the "Tough Love" institutes, a major technique is to forge contracts between parents and errant children. They appear to work well. Contract agreements, thus, rather than being cold, can stimulate respect, warmth and justice.

Section Three
OBJECTIVES

CHAPTER 7 • *Goals*

An underlying premise of the Scriptures is that faith requires projection of life into the future. The believing person takes aim on particular future actions and achievements. And institutions, through their members, can practice similar faith. Management by objective becomes vital to effective business life. In similar manner, a family becomes what it means to become when it sets objectives for its future, and determines a course of action to succeed.

CHAPTER 8 • *Growth*

An implication of Scripture is that spiritual growth is likely when God is at work among His people. The principle of growth has been taken as major for businesses that are healthy. Following that perception, families relate their own growth to God's blessing upon them. Growth is not, in its ideal meaning, always related to quantitative measure, but also to qualitative.

CHAPTER 9 • *Success*

The ultimate purpose of God is to succeed in His plan for the redemption of creation. Success is a motivating factor for most intelligent beings. Business people work and plan so that their companies will succeed. Families also wish to succeed so they learn to manage their lives and affairs, to avoid failure.

CHAPTER 7

Goals

• **How does a business translate its purposes into goals?**

• **How does a family translate its expectations into realistic goals?**

> *We should make plans—counting on God to direct us (Prov. 16:9, TLB).*
>
> *If the Lord will, we shall live, and do this, or that (James 4:15).*

The teachings of Scripture are supportive of goal orientation. The assumption of Scripture is that human beings are goal oriented. If they were not, they would not plant their fields or begin the construction of a home. In the Gospels the warning is given that when a man wishes to build he plans carefully for the future so as to avoid embarrassment (Luke 14:28). Through planning, a builder discovers that he has enough funding and other resources to complete the structure he has projected. In another situation in the Gospels, the parable of the talents is described. The wise servants use available talents to earn others and thereby increase the value of the original investment. The servant receiving criticism was the one who had no goals and buried his talent in order to preserve it (Matt. 25:15-28).

All goal setting incurs some risk. Pascal, the eminent French philosopher, argued that men of faith gambled boldly on God: they risked themselves on God's provision, were aggressive, and dreamed great dreams. When one ceases to live in the reality of this risk, he has, in an important sense, died. The Christian's risk is glorious, in that it relates to partnership with God. It is also frightening, in that the person may fail. If he takes enough risks, he will experience some failure. However, this is not failure leading to sorrow or death, but failure leading to perseverance so he may be free to risk again. And to learn so he may succeed.

The Prophetic Mood

The Scriptures represent an attitude about the future. Much of the Bible is written to predict events that will come to pass. By touching the future, a prophet not only verifies his integrity in ministry, but he affirms the respect of deity for the most important time dimension—the future. The rainbow to Noah was a sign for the future. Abraham awakened to the future of his progeny. Joseph, in Egypt, prepared for future drouth. Moses saw the land of Israel's future, even though he was denied entry himself. Later, the prophets preached about, wrote about, and acted out the future. Jeremiah was told to buy a worthless piece of land because in the future it would have significant value (Jer. 32). Those prophets who lost their vision of the future and what they were supposed to do about it—as Jonah and Elijah did—also lost their ministries.

The Scriptures inform readers about vision. Vision stimulates the believer's interest in the future, and to discover his part in it. Vision and obedience to the Great Commission stimulated the Apostle Paul to great purposes, even to reach Rome and Spain. Driven by a belief in the return of Jesus Christ as ultimate goal for human motivation and ministry, Paul set specific goals for himself. He appears to have achieved them (Rom. 15:24).

A personal goal of nearly all Jewish persons in testamental times was to be married. Young women were betrothed at twelve or thirteen years of age, and married at sixteen. However, the Apostle Paul set the goal of singleness for himself so that he could accomplish other goals for the sake of the gospel (1 Cor. 9:5). Like Paul, we are also afforded privilege to set goals for life, family, ministry, domicile or whatever.

Business Directions

For his life to have full meaning, a person must have a faithful perception of a future direction for himself and his relationship to institutions that represent him. The owners of a business, to be successful, must know something about its future in order to know what human needs to meet, what plants to build, what materials to import, how many units to produce, whom to enlist for workers and for what tasks, to gain a perceived end.

A *purpose* (or purposes) includes general direction for an individual or institution. Purpose includes overall philosophy, attitudes, knowledge of likely problems, and related matters. Discovery of opportunity is important to purpose. From these general matters goals are formulated—long and short range—to guide the activities of the owners, the dreamers, the builders. Goals or objectives are specific and measurable, cast in time frames, designed to accomplish the purposes to which they are related. They also state or imply what the institution or individual is *not* going to do. Limitations are very important to goal setting.

Setting a Course

Companies and nations verbalize their purposes in statements, in articles of incorporation, in constitutions and by-laws, or other documents. Ultimately, specific goals or directions are determined and knit to the purposes. Refinements are then honed to meet schedules and accomplish the basic expectations of those served or of those serving the institution. The greater the refinement of these goals, the greater will be efficiency. Greater efficiency means lower costs and greater likelihood the individual, business, or institution will flourish.

Time is a vital factor in the measurement of goals. To project the time when each fact is to be in focus, when each task is to be finished, when other related matters begin and end is a major game of life that many men and women find stimulating. They carry through their businesses with the concept of management by objective to be assured the process is in control. The most accepted theory, at present, is to operate a company with objectives well thought through at every level of management. These objectives are communicated, monitored during specific periods, and evaluated.

As Henry Ford bolted together the parts of his first automobile, he learned, even before he had fully assembled his machine, that there were improvements that could be made. But if he stopped to tear down, reforge, reassemble and test each completed unit repeatedly, he would never put the nation on wheels. So he completed several models and settled on the Model T, a car he knew he could improve even as he drove it out of the shop. He fulfilled his objectives, evaluated his product and made plans for further evaluation and monitoring.

Many eminent businessmen have testified that they made, lost, and made fortunes several times before eventual success. They developed an attitude that rejected fear and learned from failure, and they always believed that mistakes, disappointments, rebuffs should be accepted as part of their journey. We might choose any one of scores of real-life situations to emphasize the point. During the early 1920s, the DeWitt Wallaces introduced a magazine. *The Reader's Digest,* in St. Paul, Minnesota. They labored diligently, publishing several issues. The project floundered, and the magazine "folded." The Wallaces knew the idea was a good one. They moved to New York, began again, learning by the first experience, and launched, out of failure, one of the most remarkable publishing enterprises ever to appear.

Marriages Need Goals

Setting goals for a marriage is vital. Perhaps the most important matter in goal setting is to believe in the process itself. Individuals often rationalize away the duty to set and follow goals. They imply there is a special spirituality in doing whatever happens, following pleasant accidents in their lives. These are caused, they say, by faith and by God. Living in this way, as one author states the matter, "they fire a bullet into the wall, and then paint a target around the hole." Claiming success in this fail-safe pattern, they actually make no goals their goal. They do not perceive the illogic that is captured in this aphorism: "He that aims at nothing hits it every time."

Goals and Differences in Persons

The achievement of goals relates to bringing all details together to gain a projected end within a specified period of time. This amount of money saved within this schedule; that piece of property purchased at a specific time; this education earned in five or six years; that opportunity won before the year is out; these children born in five years; and all the rest, in combination, make a family special and move it to higher levels of accomplishment than would have been the case without objectives.

Problems of health, depression, unhappiness, differences, setbacks, doubts, neglect, and the like can be accommodated in the planning process. They may force delays, changes, shifts, acceptances, but these problems are the fallen trees in the way, the heavy snowfall, the harsh winds. A marriage is affected by them all, but a couple need not be stopped by them, or permit them to destroy the marriage. The husband and wife determined to see their marriage through to the end will build a solid family structure. In the end they will be gratified by what they have done.

A marriage builds memories and traditions. If, early in a marriage, a couple decides what memories they wish to build, the husband and wife make an ideal beginning. They set up a program to achieve what they wish to remember later on. These goals help minimize differences of opinion. They permit tolerance, if properly understood. But by setting a pattern they are not called upon to tolerate as many differences as nongoal-oriented couples.

Goals and Self-Interest

Perhaps the greatest enemy of the late twentieth-century family, as well as other institutions, is self-interest. Too great focus of self leads to unrealistic expectations, especially about persons closest to us, but they go beyond family and neighbors. We may have unreal expectations for ourselves. We are spoiled. The ease of life, especially in technologically advanced countries, has made possible the shift in this century from fighting for human survival to scurrying for excess. For centuries families held together, if for no other reason than that their members needed one another.

Families banded their members together because family and community were necessary for protection, cultural improvement, and even education. The individual had few options within that narrow community. If he wished, he could escape to the frontier. But by 1900 nature's frontiers had largely run out, at least for the masses. Forbidding tundras and unexplored space remained for only a few, and those were not really free of restraint.

New technology, harnessed in the twentieth century, has provided large incomes for workers. In spite of socialists' arguments to the contrary, laborers do not have to own the means of production to gain upward mobility. The middle class has ballooned in size. Women and minorities have been afforded more of their natural rights. The emphasis has changed from plural to singular interests. Formerly the emphasis was on "our" family, and "we" will do the job. Focus has now turned to self-interest—"I" am my own person, and what is in it for "me"? This egoism—some call it the new narcissism—has presented problems with which older institutions have not had to cope. Required long-term commitments such as traditional marriage solidarity guaranteed in a legal contract are made to appear old-fashioned. Many think that individuals can move into and out of relationships as easily and freely as they wish.

Self-interest, even when an individual chooses marriage, creates larger tensions for marriage than formerly. Expectations for personal affluence, sensuality, freedom, privilege, gain ground even in men and women who feel themselves to be traditional in their thought and conduct patterns. In many situations the inflation of expectations becomes too great. Wives or husbands sometimes feel they are being cheated, or repressed, or denied, and they rebel. They want out. Separation and divorce, and intimate relationships without marriage or responsibility, become more common. Even among conservative and traditional families divorce has increased.

When the marriage institution is evaluated by married persons, and by persons once married, the results show that those who remain married hold more realistic expectations than those who separate and divorce. Those who make solid marriages seem more concerned about other members of the family—spouse and children—than themselves. This does not mean there is insufficient self-esteem. There is a significant other-love balancing self-love. There is less selfishness.

If relevant film and television programs, as well as news stories related to unsatisfactory and broken marriages, were analyzed, one would be impressed by the number of first-person pronouns used by unhappy spouses. They accept their own opinions about divorce—that their children will not be hurt, that their actions mean nothing to society, that what "I" wish to do is the important and right thing, at least for "me." One revolts at this high degree of self-indulgence, experienced at the expense of other family members, especially children.

Goals and Expectations

Human beings are actively imperfect. Nearly everything is in some way negative for them. They glance at each other in disapproving ways. They do not keep their promises. They waste money. They get dirty, and sometimes remain dirty and smell. They snore. Some "slurp" when they eat. On occasion they are crude, and often lazy. Most work, some do not. Some are morose and/or silent around family members. Others yell. The most common reason for a person losing his job is that he cannot get along with other workers. A mate may not care for sexual intimacy. The other seems excessive in demands. Sooner or later in a family one or more members become ill and make life difficult for healthy ones. People become depressed and are hard to live with. They are suspicious, even when all others strain to please them. They grow old and die. Sometimes loved ones are relieved at the deaths of their elders. On other occasions they are angry that the dead have been so thoughtless as to die. All this relates to the human condition. The catalog of aggravations would be dictionary thick if all complaints were listed.

But most of us refuse to accept human weakness. We expect so much more. When we do not receive in reality our expectations, we soon discover we want out or we want some other radical change, but it is often a change that will not occur without undesired human cost.

It has been my privilege for many years to counsel students before they marry. After I have won their confidence and am assured that they believe my love for them, I strike hard at the problems they will face. A significant one relates to unrealistic expectations. No matter how they allege understanding, I insist they do not know what marriage is going to be like. This marriage, between these two persons, will be unique. No other marriage has ever been or ever will be quite like this one. There is no standard chart for a particular marriage. Each marriage must make its way over unbroken terrain. The going will not be easy. Nothing is automatic, no matter how carefully the relationship is assembled. Feelings always get in the way.

General uncertainty, however, does not mean that we cannot know some things well in advance. There is much to be learned from a seasoned mountain climber, even though I am going to scale a cliff that he has not climbed.

Knowledge of a method makes it possible to discover a way in the wilderness. No one can show me the way. He can only teach me a method to find my own way, and encourage me to proceed. Because our emotions never match, the journey we take will never mean quite the same thing to either of us, even when the route is the same for both.

Among the first principles of maturity are acceptance of and adjustment to that which is available. When I am willing to accept the facts of my situation, I am on my way to gaining a sense of well-being about who I am and where I am going. I begin by working with the people and resources available to me. It is an old concept: acceptance of reality. Either I curse the rocks and throw them about the field, or collect them and build a wall, or a fireplace, or a shelter. It might be better if there were more and varied materials, but no others are available. Adaptation, flexibility, substitution are virtues of human will and conduct—in business, or government, or other personal relationships. Once I realistically situate myself, I can work for new goals, explore new territory.

Goals and Risks

Two imperfect persons join their lives. If they wish to do so, and are dedicated to a common purpose, they presume that they may accomplish more together than they could as individuals. They force their dreams into practical analysis. Fantasies are weakened or changed through rejection of that which is unrealistic. Proper hopes and dreams are broken down into parts. When all usable parts are well assembled—an effort that could take three, five, ten, fifteen, and even more years to accomplish—the couple will be pleased with the results. They work and wait for those results. Waiting means they take some risk—together.

If understandings and attitudes are rightly set, the risk of purposes and goals will guarantee excitement, growth, intensification of love, adventure and meaning for a couple and, later, for their children. To fail in some of life's purposes should not be so threatening as most people make it. Failure destroys if it is permitted to do so, but for those who understand it, failure teaches, suggests change, offers release for something new.

Couples who set goals make a map for a journey, a journey worth taking if they determine both to give honor to God and to improve themselves. They will likely discover that they are enjoying themselves.

Reading about Goals and the Family

Authors with Christian or generally Christian emphases:

Alexander, John W. *Managing Our Work.* Downers Grove, Ill.: Inter-Varsity Press, 1975. 2nd revised edition.

Berry, Jo. *The Happy Home Handbook.* Old Tappan, N.J.: Revell, 1976. (pp. 81-90.)

Lee, Mark W. *How to Have a Good Marriage.* Chappaqua, N.Y.: Christian Herald, 1978. ("What are your personal and family goals?" pp. 179-83.)

————. *How to Set Goals and Really Reach Them.* Beaverlodge, Alberta: Horizon House, 1978.

————. *Our Children: Our Best Friends.* Grand Rapids: Zondervan, 1970. (pp. 90-117.)

Schaeffer, Edith. *What Is a Family?* Old Tappan, N.J.: Revell, 1975.

Authors with secular or generally secular emphases:

Naisbitt, John. *Megatrends.* New York: Warner Books, 1982.

CHAPTER 8

Growth

- **What is growth for a business?**

- **What is growth for a family?**

*As arrows are in the hand of a mighty man; so are
the children of thy youth. Happy is the man that hath
his quiver full of them (Ps. 127:4-5).*

*Not as though I had already attained, either were
already perfect: but I follow after, if that I may ap-
prehend that for which also I am apprehended of Christ
Jesus.
Brethren, I count not myself to have apprehended: but
this one thing I do, forgetting those things which are behind, and reaching forth unto those things which are
before,
I press toward the mark for the prize of the high calling
of God in Christ Jesus (Phil. 3:12-14).*

Growth is a major topic of conversation for modern man.
Analysts discuss the problems and benefits related to
growth in populations, in institutions, in nearly every
feature of society and nature. Change in numbers has often
been the most important consideration. More and more
attention is being paid to improvement of quality, as well
as, and sometimes in place of, quantitative increases.

Growth as a Biblical Concept

Spiritual growth has been, at least from the time of

Abraham, a biblical teaching. If we knew more about
Noah and his times, we might trace the concept earlier
than Abraham. The Scriptures give some attention to
growth in numbers, quantity, but have much to say about
righteousness, quality. At the time of Moses, a tribe of
people numbering perhaps one million souls was called to
live by God's commandments. They were to be a holy
people. Although Israelites carried a mission task
(proselytizing), their first duty was to live and improve
within the revelation of righteousness presented in the Old
Testament. The nations of the world would come to them,
see the maturity of their faith and conduct, and return to
recite the blessing of Jehovah to their own people (2 Chron.
9:23). The most dramatic example is that of the Queen of
Sheba who journeyed to Jerusalem to observe Solomon's
experience. She was impressed to make her own witness
of what she saw (2 Chron. 9:1-12).

In the New Testament the Church is commissioned to
evangelize, to go into all the world and preach. The
addition of churches and converts was introduced as a
concept of growth (Acts 12:24; 19:20; 1 Cor. 3:6). But the
quantitative aspect did not displace the long-standing
qualitative factors. They existed and continue to exist
together. The Apostle Paul exemplifies the dual perception
of growth. He wished to plant churches, but he also
wished to accent the importance of growing up to the full
man in Christ (Eph. 4:15). The apostle was concerned that
faith should grow (2 Cor. 10:15). The Apostle Peter also
presented the perception of spiritual growth (2 Pet. 3:18).

The concept of growth (maturation) was a major factor
in the experience and teachings of Paul (Phil. 3:8-21). If a
Christian does not perceive or hold to the concept of
growth ("attitude"), he needs further illumination (v. 15).
The high standard requires improving performance demonstrating spiritual growth (v. 16). This can be learned most
readily through observation of excellent Christian models
(v. 17).

Some evidences of spiritual growth are to be found in

family life. Israel had always believed that evidence of
God's approval on husband and wife was the birth of
children, even many children. Women like Sarah and
Hannah wondered why God left them barren. How did
they fail Him? A sign of God's approval on Job, following
his long ordeal, was the restoration of family with seven
sons and three daughters as he had at the beginning (Job
1:2; 42:13). His wealth was doubled, an impressive growth
(Job 1:3; 42:12). Increase in prosperity was taken as
indication of God's approval on His people. Decrease was
taken as evidence of disapproval.

In the New Testament the general principle is further
refined that family quality is evidence not only of God's
blessing but also of Christian maturity, obedience and
leadership. The theology of family is woven into Scripture
(Rom. 7:1-3; Eph. 5:1). If the concepts are also demonstrated in the reader's experience, the witness of Christ is
more effectively transmitted than would otherwise be the
case. One who grows spiritually will, among other
evidences, show his maturity, or attempt to do so, in
remaining married to one wife, in managing his home well,
in maintaining his children in a dignified manner, and in
knowing that failure in these matters rightly raises
questions that may require answers for potential leaders (1
Tim. 3:2-5).

A modern reader might wish that the Apostle Paul, and
other writers, would have provided more detail to the large
analogy of marriage and family to Christ and the Church,
to management and leadership, to spiritual maturity and
effectiveness, but they did not. We have sufficient
information to detect that a father role requires the man to
be tough and tender, to be competent and wise, to know
and live righteousness. For the Christian, this means
knowing and following the Scriptures.

Even the non-Christian may accomplish high purposes
because he broadens his personal perception, perhaps
religious in nature, to all that he does. He is the same in
his business as in his home. In running his business in

Japan, "Matsushita behaved as a tough shop foreman, a demanding father, *and* a gentle, philosophizing, allowing grandfather . . . Matsushita's ability to present his people with a wide range in behavior made it possible for them to fashion a view of his style that directed their attention to productivity, satisfaction, and growth: complex outcomes that he valued" (Pascale and Athos 1981, 280-81).

Many Christians in American society compartmentalize their lives. Family is segregated from business life; even church is sometimes segregated. Ideas, ideals and activities are sometimes segregated from each other. Educational institutions, with all the respect they receive, are often perceived as nests for woolly-headed theoreticians, impractical in real life. The marketplace means, to those limited to profit criterion, growth in volume by whatever means are available. Ideas and ideals mean nothing if profitable volume does not increase. Those who hold to such views will not experience growth, or wholeness, as the Scriptures suggest and the example of family solidarity implies.

Changing Concepts of Business Growth

Until recent times the concept of growth in an economy was a basic perception, easily measured. The number of laborers, rate of production, volume of products, increase in sales, and the like were taken as indicators of growth in business and barometers of potential success. They still are. Although not exclusive measurements, they continue nevertheless to be foremost indicators in nearly all businesses. Quarterly reports to stockholders are designed to reveal increases (or decreases) in production and income with resultant increases (or decreases) in gross sales, net earnings, and profits per share of outstanding stock.

During recent years traditional concepts of growth have been restudied. An awareness of limited natural resources, of weakness in unexamined affluence and materialism, of vital environmental factors, of saturation in some goods, of concern for values in the use of time and materials—all

have raised public questions about volume growth. And
these relate in some way to ethical considerations
reviewed in a later chapter of this book, but growth is an
issue to be treated discreetly from other issues.

Gradually the concept of business growth is shifting
somewhat for many to mean growth in quality, in social
application of the products of an industry, in improvement of methods and means, in ability to manage "steady
state" situations. For example, schools once reliant on
ever-expanding student enrollments were faced by 1976
with "no growth" or "low growth" freshman classes. Many
declined from former highs. Overbuilt, overstaffed, over-
projected colleges—and colleges are properly perceived as
businesses—have either adapted or have been forced to
close their doors. New breeds of managers have been
sought, men and women who can flourish in "no growth"
situations. The assignment of "no growth" analysts to
leadership positions means that the numbers game is no
longer the only consideration. The worth of a college
cannot be measured annually by larger numbers of
students enrolling. Growth, generally measured by volume or quantitative increases, has shifted to quality
improvements for educational institutions. Quality
improvement in faculty and students becomes more
important as indicators of "growth." Even the various
government levels are trying to find ways to consolidate
services with more efficient and smaller staffs. This, too,
is seen as growth in sophisticated management.

Some manufacturers recognize that growth in quality
may be the most beneficial. They learn that making half as
many units significantly improved in quality may assure
their corporations longer life, higher reputation and,
perhaps, greater profits than formerly they experienced.
Such practices may well contribute to conservation of
resources, a vital matter for the world's future. Following
World War II, Japanese manufacturers shifted from shoddy
products to high quality in one generation. Recent history
records the excellent results of that shift for Japan, and its

challenge to other nations to follow the pattern.

Family Development as Growth

Family growth has generally been related to the physical size of a family. A family, two persons in number, have a child. They become three, then four, perhaps more. At some point growth, as it is measured by the number of persons in the family, ends. Adult children leave home and the parents remain.

Growth perception does not relate only to the physical development of offspring from infants, to children, to youths, to adults. The dramatic introduction of children into a home is more than that. The generally happy experience of parenthood (if rightly engaged) must include another growth idea—commitment to child and personal development. The growth or development of the parent is part of the story.

Parents adapt to development stages in various ways, depending upon the stage and the parents. Physical changes are observed in the year-by-year development of the child—crawling and walking, occurring together with developing dexterity. Physical size increases. Changes also register in other ways, as in the appearance of teeth, loss of these and growth of a permanent set. The onset of puberty is observed in voice and body changes, hair growth, and biological cycles. All factors relate to the growth or maturing process, and require parental help to shape the attitudes, conduct and education of the child.

Each new plateau of development is more fulfilling if the previous one has been cultivated properly. For example, if discipline of the infant has been appropriate and well directed, the child, even as a toddler, will be prepared to interact meaningfully with other children. Perhaps the general failure of parents to manage adolescents is the consequence of poor preparation during the first years of their children's lives. Development of anything must adapt or build upon whatever precedes it. A business may not neglect its first years of existence and expect the later ones to be trouble free.

Many parents, principally fathers, are not sufficiently interested in working out the complex problems related to child development. They expect the family to manage itself. Many teachers state that they have never seen the fathers of some of the children they teach, even though special programs, open houses, interview periods, and parent-teacher meetings are provided. Fathers commonly show great interest in athletics, especially if their sons are players, but personal and academic matters may be totally avoided. Law enforcement officers often complain that they cannot arouse the father's interest in a truant son. The truant becomes public responsibility. I became something of a celebrity in one of my children's classes when it was discovered that I was the only father who, during the entire year, had signed the periodic grade report sent home to parents.

Discipline, appropriate and well-designed, has nearly disappeared in some families. One of the most common complaints offered by college freshmen has been: "My father didn't care enough for me to teach or practice discipline in our home." When asked what statements their fathers made to them that they most remembered, the college students listed them for the pollsters. The top three were:

"There's not enough money for that."
"I'm too tired."
"Keep quiet."

Growth and Quality

In simpler times than the present, families generated children, reared them by meeting their basic needs, and yielded to them when parents grew old. Plain food, few clothes, little education, daily chores, simple pleasures, and some religion made up the general provisions of parental duty. Some modern families believe that pattern is adequate for rearing children in the closing years of the twentieth century. It might be if society would permit, but it does not. In nearly every area, except religion, the state or some other institution has taken over responsibility to guarantee satisfaction of the needs of children.

A child requires so much more than he did formerly. He will likely be candidate for medical attention unknown to his former counterparts, for costly and lengthy education, for private accumulations of personal property, for expensive services and social involvement. To realize success for this investment, parents must take considerable interest, and become involved in all aspects of family life. That is, unless they abdicate parenthood.

How may family growth be measured in an age fostering small families? That growth must be registered, as suggested in the analogy to business, in qualitative factors. Mother and father may improve themselves in the quality of the product—both themselves and their children.

Families may well adopt this concept of quality growth. During future generations parents may be called on to devote more time and investment to one child than several children received before the twentieth century. The education of a son or daughter today often costs more than was available for all purposes to a couple in a lifetime on the American frontier. Growth has become a more sophisticated process. Professional development of both mates, limiting the number of children commonly to two, discovering individual talents and potentialities, providing training and advanced education for few children—by these means families have opened up new avenues for their energies.

Improvement for all the family members takes time. That sufficient leisure time is available for personal improvement among the masses is seen in the increased interest in spectator sports, in television viewing, as well as in other popular distractions. Perhaps some of the massive amount of time devoted to transient pleasures, no matter how legitimate some of those pleasures may be, should be given to cumulative experiences for intellectual, physical, spiritual and social growth for the benefit of the individual and his or her family.

In my observation of happy and effective men and women, I feel confident in making the following generalizations:

1.   They have a devotional life that absorbs and applies biblical materials.

2.   They have devised means for service so that they act in worthwhile ways without expectation of personal return.

3.   They have sufficient self-esteem that they can afford to affirm their mates, children and colleagues in professional and social ways.

4.   They have institutional relationships (including memberships) through which they express their ideals.

5.   They have objectives for their lives, some of which force them to do things they might neglect doing—like reading fine literature.

6.   They have an appreciation for their work, their livelihood, affording it enough time, but not too much.

7.   They have an ability to love and be loved.

8.   They have good sense about fiscal matters, making them generous but also causing them to plan intelligently for their own retirement.

9.   They have an insight into the blessings and dangers of each stage of life so that appropriate attitudes and actions are taken to help themselves and members of their families.

10.   They have an ability to say "yes" or "no" based on reasonableness without feeling guilty for taking time, or not taking time, to do something requested of them.

11.   They have a sense of humor that both gives and receives an appropriate joyfulness.

12.   They have a modest but active motivation underlying their lives—"How may I make things better, for myself and others?"

In these possessions happy people find *growth*.

Reading about Growth and the Family

Authors with Christian or generally Christian emphases:

Claypool, John. *Stages.* Waco, Tex.: Word, 1977.
Lee, Mark W. *How to Have a Good Marriage.* Chappaqua, N.Y.: Christian Herald, 1978. ("Do you plan on having children?" pp. 137-41; "What is your feeling on birth control?" pp. 141-44.)
_____. *Who Am I and What Am I Doing Here?* Milford, Mich.: Mott Media, Inc., 1982. ("What is the process?" pp. 19-43; "What is the secret?" pp. 135-44.)

Authors with secular or generally secular emphases:

Howard, Jane. *Families.* New York: Simon & Schuster, 1978.

CHAPTER 9

Success

- **What is the significance of success in business?**

- **What is the meaning of success for a family?**

What is man . . . for thou hast made him a little lower than the angels, and hast crowned him with glory and honour. Thou madest him to have dominion . . . (Ps. 8: 4-6).

Be strong and of a good courage . . . that thou mayest observe to do according to all the law . . . that thou mayest prosper whithersoever thou goest . . . for then thou shalt make thy way prosperous, and then thou shalt have good success (Josh. 1:6-8).

Success must be related to the achievement of goals. Any accomplishments, no matter how gratifying and pleasant, that are not the result of precedent goals, cannot be taken as evidences of success. Success is the accomplishment of previously determined expectations, activities, outcomes. This is difficult enough for an individual to plan and to conclude a course of action for a desired end. It is more difficult in a business or family where individual achievement must contribute to the good of the larger group. At the same time, the group's success is based on the accomplishment of its members. The goals of the group and of the individuals must be compatible with each other.

Biblical Success Patterns

The Scriptures speak to the success of all men. In some passages this concept is cast as prosperity. To be successful with God, presumed the Old Testament writers, was to be prosperous. The psalmist wrote: *I have been young, and now am old; yet have I not seen the righteous forsaken, nor his seed begging bread* (Ps. 37:25). In a conversation I once had with the late W. F. Albright, the eminent Palestinian archaeologist, regarding dating of materials, he told me, "It is fairly easy for dating biblical materials to relate high spiritual and political performance with prosperity. When Israel developed spiritual and political qualities, as they did under David and Solomon, the pottery is well-formed and artistically finished. When Israel was in deep decline, the relics reflect the condition of the people—the pottery was poorly made, poorly fired, and unpainted."

In spite of this rather practical view that rising affluence is evidence of success, and decline is evidence of failure, there are other biblical measures for success that are more important for men and women of Christian faith. Success is at the end of something, not at the beginning. Terah set out from Ur of Chaldees to win a new land. Had Abram wandered about and stumbled upon the land, taking it for his own, he would not have been successful. He would have been fortunate, or we might say, "Providence smiled on him."

Success in life is related to faith projections into the future, and following them up for a lifetime. At least two acts are necessary for success: (1) to make a commitment, and (2) to achieve the commitment. If Jesus made the commitment to live a life of selflessness by which He had no house, no pillow, no wealth, and if He carried through on that commitment to accomplishment, He succeeded. If He had become wealthy, constructed a palace, and wore rich clothing, He would have failed. To succeed one does what he says he will do.

The Scriptures hold a broad concept of success that fits the particular faith commitment to the actual achievement. Abraham's servant made a commitment to his master, swearing to him that he would carry out the purpose to find a wife for Isaac in the distant land. Knowing what he must do, the servant in arriving at Nahor prayed, *O Lord . . . grant me success today . . .* (Gen. 24:12 NASB). His success was achieved when, meeting and persuading Rebekah, the servant returned to his master with the young woman.

It appears that success is only partially understood, either during biblical times or currently. In the event of success there is purpose, even if it is evil purpose, that when fulfilled means success. All other human activity relates to accidents, pleasant or tragic, for which assignment of responsibility is somewhat difficult.

To be rich, as Nabal was, was not perceived as success by his wife Abigail, or by neighbors who found him churlish, or even by David who found him unappreciative. In the end, near his death, even Nabal must have perceived that he had succeeded in one sense, but missed in that which counted (1 Sam. 25:37).

That the Scriptures attach great value to the right success there can be no doubt. Success is in quality of life, finding patterns to follow that preserve family, health, work and devotion, and following them through to the end. At the end, one may evaluate his activity and determine the degree of his success or failure.

There is little in Scripture that implies that success is an exciting matter. There may be excitement on occasion, but the prevailing mood is deep satisfaction when one has done what he ought to do, and the greatest satisfaction is that one has pleased the Lord, has benefited others, and has evaded inordinate pride. To be successful while maintaining humility is an ideal of high order for the Christian.

Business Success and Life

In her book on success, *How to Get Whatever You Want Out of Life,* Joyce Brothers clusters factors that predominate in successful people. Summarizing numerous studies of success in business, she discovered, among other factors, that highly successful men had "dull" marriages. They were likely to be married to their first wives, and their marriages were presumed to be solid. The author pointed out that the marriages did not have to be dull for the men to be successful.

In reading the analysis one becomes unsure about the definition of a "dull" marriage. Perhaps general expectations for marriages are somewhere in a fantasy Disneyland. When all factors are combined in life, marriage may not appear exciting. It may not yield to the meaning of excitement, as that concept is popularly understood. Its solidarity makes a difference for good in the general society. It may provide personal satisfaction that cannot be measured. It might be more gratifying than the Brothers citation would reveal.

While not all successful men have solid marriages, it is true that men who permit contradiction in their personal and business standards set themselves up to fail both in their marriages and their businesses. A success/failure ambivalence can thwart them in nearly everything they do or ought to do. Often I have been asked by wives to explain husbands who seem to want to be married and not want to be married at the same time. The husband will not keep even a semblance of schedule in the home. He violates family interests, disregards his duties to wife and children, and finds domestic life too confining. Yet he may groom himself well, keep company with other women, and develop interesting hobbies.

He defends his actions, claiming that he lives for his wife and children, buys them gifts, spends days with them in happy exchange, and meets their financial needs. He is jealous of them and expects high levels of conduct from them. He would not countenance his wife following similar patterns of his conduct outside the home. He will some-times criticize his own attitudes and actions, does not want a divorce, and claims he will someday straighten out his personal conduct. He is irritated that his wife is not patient about matters.

In business this man, as boss, seldom permits pro-fessional contradictions that parallel the domestic ones he blissfully follows. He might show his impatience with such conduct in various ways, including direct protest to of-fenders. He might terminate their employment. But in marriage he does not recognize, or does not acknowledge, the similar principle that when contradictions are per-mitted to compete, the situation is on the way to being lost—albeit slowly lost. Failure will follow in time. Loyalty has been dissolved. Other virtues have also been lost so that, by our definition, the man cannot succeed. Success, as we interpret it ethically, adds benefit for all who relate to it: it does not subtract.

During the late nineteenth century many large companies grew into great corporations. The moguls of early industry were men who, in most instances, rose from poverty to riches by dint of individualism, hard work, opportunism, skill, privilege, and low cost labor. They rode the first tide of an expanding technology. They perceived themselves as virtuous in at first winning and then holding on to their gains, although many felt uneasy about their success at the expense of so many exploited citizens. Some, like Andrew Carnegie, tried to give back some of their "success." Carnegie, by building libraries in various communities, presumed that he had returned his wealth to people and therefore relieved his concern about the concentration of so great wealth in individual hands.

This concept of high profits accruing to a few persons as the great mark of success has only gradually, and some-times grudgingly for some, given way to the larger per-ception that success includes profits, and happy partici-

pating workers, and social advancement, including hus-
banding care of nature and economy of resources. Success
only comes to us, if at all, when purposes are determined,
and legitimate, genuine effort given to them for achievement. More and more the serious literature of business
includes the larger picture, a success that is less selfish
but more satisfying than mere volume growth.

Among the highly successful businessmen who contended for success to be measured by larger motives than
money making was Joyce C. Hall, founder of Hallmark, Inc.
In his autobiography, *When You Care Enough,* he wrote:

> If a man goes into business with only the idea of making
> a lot of money, chances are he won't. But if he puts
> service and quality first, the money will take care of
> itself. Producing a first-class product that is a real need
> is a much stronger motivation for success than getting
> rich.

When the browser looks through the popular titles under
the *Business* section of the modern bookstore in a shopping
mall, he is rightly appalled at the brashness, egotism, irresponsibility of many popular authors. During the 1970s
and into the 1980s, the titles suggested: (1) try get-rich-
quick schemes, especially through manipulation of other
people's money, principally in precious metals or real
estate; (2) avoid taxes through shelters, such as making
purchases of certain kinds of assets, or playing the loop-
holes; (3) follow patterns recommended in the stock
market, especially in some exotic issues; (4) make an aggressive approach to others so that you can, by confrontation, get what you want. It is little wonder that "business," as the word is popularly used, gains poor reputation.

The best businesses are concerned about success with
people—the people who work for them, the people who
purchase their services or products, and the remaining
people affected by the results. The business that is most

concerned to set ideal purposes to serve the whole society, and which tenaciously follows those purposes to achievement in their own special way are the most successful, as we understand the meaning of the word.

Family Success Means All Members Win

The most sensible concept of human success, we have argued, is to set a goal and achieve it. That person who does so perceives himself to be successful who wins the game he joins, gains the girl he goes after, obtains the job against competition he sets out to beat. In the nature of things a winner often gains what someone else does not have but would like to have. In this sense success can be at the expense of another, even if the expense is modest like the mere disappointment of a parlor game loser. In business, to capture a larger percentage of the market means that a competitor must accept a lower percentage. There is no more than 100 percent of any market. In virtually any situation elements of selfishness are ever-present and must be kept in check by the rules of the game. In competition there is at least one, and sometimes there are several or many losers.

Success is sometimes perceived in the terms noted above and no others—winners and losers. Little wonder that for many people success has gained a doubtful reputation. In this context it is selfish, a gain for one that subtracts from, and may exact too much of a loss from, another.

Not all success, however, is at a competitive level in which for every winner there is at least one loser. Success may also relate to gaining values, goals, approval, and the like in any venture. To be successful means to set and achieve my own goals, direction, and ideals. Any competition should be self-related—achieving my goals or not achieving them. That competition is *within* me, not between me and someone else. I become my own competition—my own champion or my own enemy. It is up to me to set standards and follow courses so that "I" as champion overcome "I" as opponent. The competition is between my performance without direction and my performance with direction. Only if I have perceived direction will I know if I have succeeded or failed. Such success adds benefit for all: it does not subtract. It is in this sense that success is honorable as used in its ideal here.

Careful attention to the nature and products of culture tell us much about the quality of the people—what they believed, how their families fared, and why they rose or fell in historical periods. An analyst, in the future, will have much to say about the quality of current business, education, marriage and the family, or the government in the United States and Canada. He will be able to make judgment because of prevailing and clear evidence left behind. For the generations of the late twentieth century he may note great successes—like space travel, energy development, communications and manufactures, especially in electronics.

However, among the negatives, analysts will likely suggest that failures of marriage and parenting—evidenced by such statistics as the divorce rate, by the plaintive stories and ordeals of youths, by the nature of popular arts and entertainments, by the language patterns, by the crime levels and ages of criminals, by the sexual mores, and the like—were among the social/cultural failures of the era, rivaled only by warfare. And those analysts will likely say that things did not have to follow the pattern they did. The people refused their own wisdom.

Success Takes Time

Success must be cast within a time frame. Sports provide a specific analogy for timing, for they are a microcosm of standard business enterprise, even of life itself. A football game lasts for sixty minutes of playing time. This is divided into quarters so that progress may be measured partly by the expenditure of time as well as by the score on the board. As time runs out, the game changes to fit the circumstances of the remaining minutes. The team in the lead stalls to permit minutes, even seconds, to "run out." The losing team shifts tactics, steps up its own play, using "times out" and the like. Each team attempts to use the clock to achieve success.

A marriage deserves the full time required to gain success. A couple moves from one context of feeling to another, almost inevitably. As a marriage flows from early innocence, passion and idealism into the period of reality, recovery of individuality and resulting competition between mates, one or both partners may drop out, call off or forfeit the game. Another quarter may never be permitted to start, even though winning is clearly possible. Unfinished, the game means frustration for everyone.

Most divorced persons, about 80 percent, say a year or so after the granting of the decree that they wish they had not divorced. One reason for this second thought is that, like coaches and players after a loss in a game, they see where they could have made different moves, introduced new plays, and won the contest. If they had only remained to the end, success would have been more likely than defeat. Dropping out assured defeat. As can be done in a game, they forfeit. They must take a loss. They defeated themselves. The opposition took no genuine honor or laurels.

Willingness in the partners to bear the trying construction years is helpful to the preservation of a marriage. It takes years of fumbling, of losing some yards, of missing kicks and passes before the family team will win consistently.

Uniqueness Wins

The dominant characteristic of successful persons emerging from the studies cited by Joyce Brothers is uniqueness. The concept of uniqueness is an old one, appearing long before current evidence proved its importance. Russell Conwell repeated his basic speech, "Acres of Diamonds," during a period of fifty years. A key thought in the speech was that a business person should be sufficiently alert to discover a community need that no one else was meeting—and meet it. To be alone in doing something needed would, said Conwell, guarantee success, success which he largely cast in terms of money wealth.

An unusual example of this truth is seen in the skill provided by "Red" Adair, who, at the time of this writing, has become something of a personality, sought by the news media for interviews. His uniqueness is that he and his men extinguish oil well fires more effectively than anyone else in the western world. He once stopped a fire on a rig in the North Sea that had raged for days. Within hours he was on his way to another part of the world to put out a fire no other professional could handle. Adair and his crew possess a unique skill. That places them in special situations where they succeed.

Uniqueness is also highly valued in educational circles. Every doctoral candidate defending his dissertation feels like a unique person. No one knows as much about the narrowed subject as he does. The specialist moves upward in his mastery of a specific area of a larger field until he is in demand for the special information he knows that few others or no one else possesses.

In my view, every marriage should have some feature about it resembling or feeling like uniqueness. In reading about families, one is impressed how great is the solidarity in families molded together by some special interest identifying them. In the circus world, families have for generations maintained loyalty to themselves because members were dedicated to tightrope walking or being shot from cannons. Not all participated in the same way—some took care of costumes, some erected apparatus, some cared for family needs, and some made public appearances. But all were held together by something special relating to their family name.

Several families of my acquaintance love to ski together, avidly developing the sport. Some do not ski, but they find satisfaction in some way in the environment. One family I know has started sky diving, but not all want to parachute. Self-grounded members wrap chutes and provide an enthusiastic audience. Another family is made up of concert-goers. Careful planning, budgeting and researching go into the family project. Schedules run for a year or so in advance. Special meals are planned, at home or elsewhere, for concert nights.

One of the reasons why evangelical church-going families possess a significantly better record than average for marriage is that church interests serve as means for intensification of family relationships. The nature of the church—its teachings, its people, its building, its activities—helps create that special feeling. In my experience in the churches I have attended, few couples have obtained divorces. To have done so would have meant to run in the face of friends, loved and admired, whose opinions were respected. For families like these, Christian faith and church identity create what I term *intense mutuality*. (The above does not deny that, by the 1970s there was a scandalous rise in divorce rates in evangelical churches, but the problem included fewer persons than seemed to be the case.)

Preparation for the intensely mutual activity, if carried out with appropriate attitudes, creates good feelings among family members. Our family held a pattern for getting ready for church. Everyone would rise, enjoy leisurely time together, have breakfast, get dressed up, crowd into the car, and go to church. Some families, I have discovered, make the period a miserable time, screeching at one another, implying that church is a duty rather than a privilege and will be dull anyway. We refused to let that happen. Our purpose was to focus on our family, our God, and our church. We created an affirmative environment.

Certainly mutuality proved to be successful for us. We followed the religious involvement of our children from their early years into adult life. When they were children, before Sunday school, they would sometimes play church, with assigned roles: one was preacher, one usher, and one, later two, the congregation. (I noticed that no offering was received.) Many years later, when our eldest child worked

for an airline, the supervisor would try to schedule her
"around" Sunday so that she would be free to go to church.
The supervisor learned how important church was to the
total well-being of our daughter. All our adult children are
now churchgoers on their own.

As a successful business focuses on the production of a
special product, so a family ought to have at least one
special focus to which all members are dedicated. For the
Christian family, this is likely to relate in some way to the
church. There can and ought to be several special traditions in a family, but one will emerge as priority. If it
does not, the family is not likely to achieve all the solidarity it should.

Reading about Success and the Family

Authors with Christian or generally Christian emphases:

Bustanoby, Andre. *You Can Change Your Personality.*
   Grand Rapids: Zondervan, 1977. (Appendix A, "Learning
   Contract," p. 163.)

Gangel, Kenneth O. *Competent to Lead.* Chicago: Moody
   Press, 1974.

Lee, Mark W. *How to Have a Good Marriage.* Chappaqua,
   N.Y.: Christian Herald, 1978. ("Do you share the same
   interests?" pp. 146-50; "How do you handle your
   partner's success or failure?" pp. 162-64.)

_____. *Creative Christian Marriage.* Pasadena, Calif.:
   Regal Books, 1977. (pp. 117-43.)

Authors with secular or generally secular emphases:

Brothers, Joyce. *How to Get Everything You Want Out of
   Life.* New York: Simon and Schuster, 1979.

Section Four
ORGANIZATION

CHAPTER 10 • *Administration*

The biblical view of administration is that order is gained through the work of leaders and followers, with rights and privileges accruing to persons following the order. Well-managed businesses assume management order to accomplish the good of persons touched by those businesses. Families using leadership principles can create order and find strength to develop effectively both their corporate families and the individual persons who make them up.

CHAPTER 11 • *Work*

The very creation is evidence that God worked. Out of the creation organized work, guided by patterns of control, was given to man in following God's example. Businesses are formed to make work profitable and to provide goods and services to improve the circumstances of life. Families follow the patterns of work, alternating between labor and rest. Work, designed by God, proceeded from Himself, to families, to the corporation, and is best when perceived in that chronology.

CHAPTER 12 • *Finances*

Wealth and its uses, by individuals or institutions, are common and important biblical themes. Without money as both a tool and motive for business, the commercial world would be moribund. Wealth creates a special kind of human dynamics. Whether in business or in a family, money must be effectively managed to accomplish purposes necessary to life and ideals.

CHAPTER **10**

Administration

- **How is a business managed?**

- **How is a family organized?**

> A bishop then must be blameless, the husband of one
> wife, vigilant, sober, of good behaviour, given to hos-
> pitality, apt to teach; Not given to wine, no striker, not
> greedy of filthy lucre; but patient, not a brawler, not
> covetous; One that ruleth well his own house, having his
> children in subjection with all gravity; (For if a man
> know not how to rule his own house, how shall he take
> care of the church of God?) Not a novice, lest being lifted
> up with pride he fall into the condemnation of the devil
> (1 Tim. 3:2-6).

Administration in Scriptures is closely coupled with
leadership principles and model life in administrators.
Failure in maintaining standards of model conduct, in the
Bible or society, sometimes causes leaders to lose their
status or positions. On still other occasions, hypocritical
leaders lose or are denied at least a portion of the reward
of their work. In skills of leadership, David or Elijah must
have improved as they grew older, but they suffered in
their administrations because of their own modeling failures. David was immoral with Uriah and Bath-sheba, and
Elijah retreated from leadership through fear of Jezebel.
Moses, in anger, struck the rock for water rather than
speak to it as he was commanded. Being fiercely angry, he
lost self-control and marred the model in an important

moment in the life of Israel. For that error he was denied entry into the promised land.

Administration in modern times commonly requires large coordination of the supplies of resources and working personnel. With little in the way of resources, biblical leaders were heavily reliant upon skill in developing interpersonal relationships to get things done. Much of the Bible narrative reviews the success and failure of leadership and interpersonal relationships, together with their meanings to the programs and lives of persons, families, nations, and the church. Those meanings were sometimes long lasting, even extending into modern times. The book of the Acts of the Apostles records some decisions of administration that remain important in the work of the church in the twentieth century. Christian confidence in leadership and church or family administration is identified with the biblical narrative. We limit our discussion to factors of interest for family administration.

Biblical Modeling

If a church may be viewed, in a sense, as a business, we can find in suggestions from the Apostle Paul a pattern similar to that proposed in this book. Perhaps the apostle would state the issues in reverse—managing a business like a family rather than managing a family like a business. The model, father/husband, as described in 1 Timothy 3, is blameless, married to one wife, vigilant, sober, well-behaved, hospitable, a teacher, is not a drunkard, is not violent, is not miserly, but is patient, is not argumentative, is not covetous, is not a novice. A novice in this context would be amateurish, inexperienced and proud.

Little wonder that the apostle affirms that this ideal leader should be one that administers his own house well. He would be a model person in leadership. This does not mean that every exemplary husband/father would make an astute business leader. Nor will every effective leader become an exemplary father. We are dealing with analogies, not laws.

Perhaps little argument against husband/father leadership appears from Christians who are committed to straightforward biblical principles of family organization. Objections come generally from those wives and children who do not have a husband/father who is a model and leader. He may demand his own privilege and shoulder his way through to the head of the family because, being a man, he presumes, provides him with authority. His attitudes, based on unearned status and unfair circumstances, create ill feeling among family members and lead to ineffective management.

Administration in a family, according to the Bible, begins with the virtue of the administrator. The farther the administrator retreats from the ideal, the less effective he may expect to be. This belief in excellence of modeling is almost universally accepted by both secular and religious analysts. Nearly all those analysts relate the husband and father to the first duty for modeling in the family.

Perhaps the most dramatic biblical model of wifely virtue is found in the story of Abigail and Nabal. In reality Abigail became the spiritual leader of her household. She led in other ways as well without violating the principle of submission. She demonstrated how wifely leadership is developed and used. It is doubtful that one can find in the Scriptures a woman more opposite from her husband than Abigail was from Nabal. Job's wife seems not to have been as much at variance with her husband as Abigail was from Nabal. Abigail was praiseworthy in her basic attitude about life and service to her husband and others. Her virtue and wisdom totally captivated David, preventing him from executing Nabal, an act that would have been appreciated by many of Nabal's acquaintances.

Abigail, through her piety and practice of family integrity, was able to maintain decency in her family. Not many persons would have blamed her for leaving Nabal, abandoning him to his deserved end. But this was her family, too. Abigail labored to make up Nabal's lack.

Vengeance, if any was to be meted out, was left in the hands of God. For Abigail, God is God and able to achieve His purposes, sometimes through the sufferings of His children. Suffering is a teacher. God's children do not run away, or connive change, but make the best of their circumstances, relying on God's grace.

Perhaps the main difference between Abigail and most moderns is that Abigail was quite willing to have God decide her responsibility. She would make the best of what had been dealt to her. Most persons are unwilling to accept that process, so they move matters along with the primary purpose of their own relief. Abigail found appropriate justification for action in her faith and confidence. The principle is more basic than we realize. Case histories teach us that many who justify themselves to break up their marriages often do not gain the relief they hoped for.

Those who vigorously protest personal injustices occurring to them might evaluate such passages as Hebrews 11, especially the latter verses. There is, and ought to be, a faith in the God who can make life's burdens bearable. It is not necessary that personal justification and easy escape be practiced by the Christian. In our time there would be a dozen rationalizations for justifying an escape from Abigail's marital ordeal. Abigail would take none of them.

Many devout women are reluctant to assume the primary leadership role in their families. If the commonly accepted exegesis of Ephesians 5:21-33 is agreed to, their reluctance is understandable. The passage relates the roles of husband and wife to those of Christ and the Church. The husband/father/maleness role is used as a leadership classification in the family, to the church, and by implication, to society. The wife/mother/femaleness role is used as a followership classification in the family, to the church, and by implication, to society. The husband role is constructed on the analogy of the husband to Christ, and the wife role on the analogy of the wife to the Church. Christ holds a leadership role to the Church, a role guided by perfect love, and the Church holds a followership role

to Christ, a role guided by perfect submission. It is a submission based on the model of perfection, not subjugation
based on response to ownership. To these two roles within
the family a third is added, the child who is obedient to
both parents. The analogy is complete: the loving Savior
(husband) in relationship with a submissive Church (wife)
generates converts (children).

Although complete, the analogy is also a mystery (5:32).
In part, that mystery means that although the uniqueness
of Christian marriage may be readily perceived in the
analogy, the analogy does not reveal everything about
either Christ and the Church, or the roles of all family
members. The roles described in Ephesians 5 break down
in individual families when a member does not maintain
the assignment for the role. If, for example, a husband is
unloving, he will not serve well in the role of the Christ
figure in the home.

The authority of a *model* leader is not based solely on
his or her sex, but is also derived from his or her virtues.
If the wife becomes the family leader, as she may and must
when the husband, on his own, retreats, fails or abandons
duty, the analogy of Christ and the Church to the Christian
family is diluted, perhaps lost to that family. The family,
even when biblical roles are confused or lost, may become
fine and workable in a secular society, but it is not the
New Testament pattern of family organization. Even the
Trinity practices role relationships for administrative
purposes that lead to order and effectiveness. The roles
were vital to Jesus' teaching: the Father (leader "father"
and final resource), the Son (offspring or "child" role of
obedience from and to the father), and the Holy Spirit
(comforting or "mother" role relating to father and son, to
nurture the children).

The Business Analogy

A business, to be successful, requires competent
management. The chief officer, and there must be one, co-
ordinates all relevant factors sufficiently well for the

corporation to survive and flourish. He must be aware of costs, labor pools, markets, and other factors. He is responsible to aid those persons dependent on him for supportive services.

The manager is at his best when he includes his people in the decision-making process. They should be mobilized in such a way that their ideas are heard and implemented. He should explain any rejection of proposals made by subordinates, but his role does include the right to reject proposals in appropriate manner. His conduct is not autocratic, nor is his position evidence of personal superiority. It is one of ultimate authority which should be related to an attitude of genuine humility and astute wisdom.

Principles of Leadership

Businesses guided by strong and insightful leadership are known to be the most effective. Other administrators and laborers tend to be happier with their work when they know that the head of their company is just and firm, is competent to make decisions, and can be counted on, especially during difficult times. In late 1978 the Chrysler Corporation hired Lee Iacocca, the outgoing president of the Ford Motor Company. Iacocca had dramatically proved his abilities in automobile design and production with the development of the Mustang model for Ford in 1965. He advanced to lead the company, but in falling-out with the chief stock controller, Henry Ford II, Iacocca was dismissed.

Chrysler, a multibillion dollar company, was floundering. Despite the wealth of the company and its stable of in-house managers, the board of Chrysler hired, at a first cost of millions, an administrator who could "bring the company together." With the name of Iacocca on its side, Chrysler gained huge concessions from labor, banks and the government. Both Canada and the United States supported the company with hundreds of millions of dollars in guarantees of loans. At this writing it remains to be seen whether the confidence placed in Iacocca was

justified. If it was not, there would be no other principle to
apply than to find an administrator who could accomplish
what the trustees expected of their president. That is to
provide administrative leadership competent to solve
gargantuan problems. If Iacocca fails, someone else must
be found who will succeed, or the incorporation fails, a
tragic possibility for thousands of employees. In any event,
the company must have adequate leadership to survive.
Four years after Iacocca took over, Chrysler appeared to be
on a survival course, and loans were scheduled for repay-
ment. The recovery appears remarkable.

Participatory Management

The ideal leader includes his followers in the process of
leadership. This is not a charade to make them feel warm
about his deference to them. It is a legitimate way of doing
things. To some the method seems slow, seems to substitute democracy for wisdom, seems to deny the traditional
perception of leadership, seems to shift responsibility.
Each of these apparent weaknesses can be answered.

The method is sometimes sluggish, but is speed always a
necessity? Sometimes it is. If decisions need to be made
rapidly, they can be. The other personnel know that delay
may be unwise or impossible. Well-run businesses combine
fast decision and participatory management processes.
Boards make decisions, but also put confidence in their administrators to use prudence for the day-to-day functioning of business life. The president makes a decision, sometimes because of circumstances, contrary to the actions of
his board. He knows that an adequate explanation is all
that is necessary to gain the support of his directors for
amending their action. If he has no explanation, the board
may reprimand the leader and insist on better conduct
from him, or perhaps remove him.

The method may seem to substitute democracy for
wisdom. But democracy and wisdom can live together, and
they should. The assumption that democracy is not
amenable to wisdom is unproven. To draw upon many

opinions is, in itself, an act of wisdom. Proverbs 24:6 states that in the multitude of counselors there is safety. On many occasions wisdom cannot be gained without democracy.

Whatever superior wisdom from an individual that may be diluted in group decision making on some occasion, is more than made up for in extensive contributions from the group on other occasions. Wisdom, whether resting in one or many persons, is likely to emerge when the wisest person utilizes the tools of justice and fairness. Those who must follow will do so more readily because of shared participation. The implementation of some ideas, even the better ones, may need to be delayed until persons are properly oriented. The right thing must also await the right time.

The participatory method may appear to deny traditional perceptions of leadership. But what tradition is meant? Biblical women were asked their opinions on various matters, including their willingness to marry. Pericles in ancient Athens reminded the nation that men did not proceed to make important decisions without counsel from their women. Who can justify the independent decision making of dictators of nations, moguls of industry, tyrants of families? Evidence is against them.

Finally, this method may seem to shift responsibility. But the person ultimately carrying responsibility is generally afforded the most significant voice in decision making. He bears responsibility but not so heavily as he might if he disregarded the persons affected by actions taken. If they have been heard, their concepts applied where possible, and the project fails, they are likely willing to accept the outcome with some equanimity, and share some responsibility.

Family Management

Many principles of business *leadership* apply to family guidance and success. There are some observable differences, of course. Failure in a family need not be permanent, nor is there any necessary reason to obtain another manager than the resident one. If help is needed, there are family counselors and others who can and will assist. If uncertain family members are willing to be assisted, their homes can flourish.

The Chairman of the Board

A family, like a business, should have someone authorized to affirm any final word in crucial matters. Doing so, that person assumes the largest responsibility for assuring success. Nevertheless, decision making is related to agreed-on policy. It is not arbitrary, but skillful, based on information available in each circumstance and related faithfully to all affected parties.

A sufficient number of guidelines may be agreed on in a family so that decisions will generally be by consensus. All parties presume that they have taken part and all have come to an action or opinion similar to that of the others. Often, even most of the time, well-made decisions are constructed in that fashion, but a few decisions require a specifically responsible person. These will devolve on the chief administrator. As a rule, those affected by such a decision will grant its wisdom. The administrator's attitudes in other multiplied experiences earn the consensus that he should make a particular decision. Because he carries greatest responsibility in a matter, he is afforded the privilege of highest authority.

That chief administrator may be the husband, the wife, or even one of their children. Authority shifts, depending on the occasion or situation. When parents live long and become feeble, one of the children commonly serves as administrator, the conservator, the trustee of the family. He may convene family members to discover corporate opinion and take steps to see that it is carried through. It is vital that a family member take on the role, because families without leadership are often misused, bilked, exploited. They are exposed to tragic possibilities and are vulnerable to attack. Families losing their leader members become objects for con artists and thieves.

Even in nature some animal species thrive or fail as their leaders thrive or fail. Bulls and rams take over herds and flocks. Lemmings follow one another off cliffs. Even whales lead other whales onto beaches. Leadership is in the "nature" of things, for good or ill.

An administrator becomes the focus for family expectations. In that person, presumably father and sometimes mother, young children find the confidence, the competition, the responsibility, the leadership model they need for personal development. General well-being is related to knowledge that a concerned, competent person is at the helm.

An ideal family may be in balance between extremes of anarchy and dictatorship, between a matrix of equals and a pyramid of authority. In *Parent Power! A Common-Sense Approach to Raising Your Children in the Eighties,* John Rosemond suggests that the family is more a hierarchy than a democracy, and the parents must have the final say. Democracy is impossible because children must learn restraints of self-sacrifice, self-control, and self-sufficiency, all necessary virtues to make democracy work. If the parents are both firm and kind, in a benevolent dictatorship, all members have some say and their viewpoints are respected. But the parents have the final word (Rosemond 1981).

The Necessity of Leadership

The general decline of public confidence in leadership is partly justified by poverty of talent in many leaders, the abdication of duty by some, and the unjustified egotism of others. Ethical and moral issues are often disregarded. But failure of leaders does not dissolve the basic need for leadership in institutions. Confusion about what it is can rob a family of leadership. Confusion arises when people believe that leadership is unnecessary, that it is a prerogative of different persons who inherit their status, or that it is invariably corrupt in some way.

Criticism of the traditional role of the husband/father sometimes grows out of the failures of men to serve their family assignments. Many only make gestures toward fulfillment of the paternal role. They are unwilling to invest themselves in family duty. The weaknesses or failures of either mate help fuel the fires of marriage faultfinding. When husbands fail, say in leadership, there arises a belief that leadership should be equalized to guarantee that something will be done to guide family fortunes and conduct. To attempt to solve the problem, some critics would dissolve leadership as a family principle. Men and women living together without formal marriage commonly state that they resist legalizing their relationship so as to avoid roles of leadership and domesticity.

A response to this criticism of traditional leadership is that nations or families can no more omit leadership from their existence and survive socially than a physical being can lose a vital organ and survive. This is Paul's logic in Romans 13, in which he defends governments, even unsatisfactory ones. Leadership is a fact of orderly existence, whether we like it or not. Nations must have presidents, kings, dictators, or commissars. When they try combinations, like equal king and queen, or a troika of citizens, or some other, a leader of leaders emerges. One is stronger in some significant way than the other or others.

Leadership in a family, as in business, can be focused on three key factors: (1) relationships with persons (sensitivity, peace, communications, fairness), (2) ability to solve problems (analysis, clear recital of the problem, understandable planning to solve it), and (3) willingness to model life for others (consistency, "other" concern, honesty, ideals). Leaders try to afford enough time to work through problems and give persons room to conclude with them in a course of action. There are, when possible, options or alternatives to be chosen or to provide amendments to initial proposals. Although there is much more to leadership; (1) effectiveness with people, in confronting inevitable problems, and (2) effectiveness in presenting an exemplary approach to life and situations, are two characteristics for excellence in administration.

Certainly other factors are important, such as energy levels in both leaders or managers, and those they supervise. An effective parent, like an effective manager, is flexible to allow time and provide help during crisis periods. There must also be some reserve so that new and immediate strategies may be formed. An attitude of optimism, of challenge to succeed, should be present.

Where husbands fail in leadership, model wives offer a solution. They are on the scene and provide important reserves when their husbands fall back or are incapacitated. Perhaps they must serve because their husbands are absent. These wives attempt to put into effect the principles illustrated in the biblical models. Their first choice, if we understand the relevant texts, is a voluntary submission to their husbands in family affairs. That principle is established in the model, is observed in the experience of Sarah, *whose daughters ye are, as long as ye do well, and are not afraid with any amazement* (1 Pet. 3:6). It is not the consequence of any alleged female weakness.

If a husband is not the leader, the mother will likely become the leader. But the point is made—*there is a leader.* It is vital that the leadership principle be recognized. Even if the leader is absent from the remaining family members, as a traveling or military father might be, the knowledge that there is a leader is enormously helpful. There ought to be a feeling of confidence that all members focus upon the leader who repays this honor by giving himself, present or absent, to the welfare of the members.

For a period of fifteen months this principle of absentee leadership was well illustrated in my family. Funding became available for me to complete a doctoral program at a university three hundred miles from our home. It was obvious that to uproot the family for my educational purposes would be unwise. Our children, four plus an additional child living with us, were well established in local schools. My wife had a job nearby at the college where I taught. The cost of moving was prohibitive.

Family members were convened to discuss options. I told the children what the situation might be, and said that I would be willing to give up the opportunity for further education. Each one, even the seven-year-old in her way, protested that we had looked forward to this goal and we could not give it up now. They tossed the problem back to me. I asked, "But if I go, who will be the father in the family? Who will help your mother carry through on all that must be done? She works and has the house duties, with five children to guide and keep at peace."

They responded magnificently. They promised to maintain family guidelines, to assist their mother, to ease inevitable pressures. And they did it. On Friday evenings, late, or early Saturday mornings, their mother gave me her report as the children sat about the kitchen table beaming with her words of praise and my approval. If during the week their mother would say, "We will discuss that with Dad, he will settle it," the children would immediately plead for reconsideration and settlement before my return. They were that responsive to their absent father and their initial promises. They did not want to be the cause for having me abandon the educational project that meant so much to everyone.

During those fifteen months, and another period later, the children, responsive to leadership, matured. They seemed to prove that they too could be responsible and become leaders, as their participation might be needed. They felt then, and continue to feel, that their father's leadership made our family a unit, gave it solidarity and direction, even when their mother was the leader in their father's absence.

The concept is basic in Christianity, where the apostle, the deacon, the elder, the bishop serve as leaders in the church in the stead of Jesus Christ, the absent Lord. The whole matter is understood in the principles of respect, humility and loyalty.

Reading about Administration and the Family

Authors with Christian or generally Christian emphases:

Berry, Jo. *The Happy Home Handbook*. Old Tappan, N.J.: Revell, 1976. (pp. 15-27.)

Engstrom, Ted W. and Edward R. Dayton. *The Art of Management for Christian Leaders*. Waco, Tex.: Word Books, 1976.

Lee, Mark W. *How To Have a Good Marriage*. Chappaqua, N.Y.: Christian Herald, 1978. ("Do you believe in careful, sensitive listening?" pp. 167-69; "Do you believe in talking over matters and sharing in decision making for the family?" pp. 170-71; "Do you understand the husband's leadership in the family?" pp. 194-98.)

CHAPTER 11

Work

- How does a business assign work among its employees?

- How does a family divide the chores of the household?

> *He who does not work shall not eat* (2 Thess. 3:10, TLB).
>
> *Six days shalt thou labour, and do all thy work* (Exod. 20:9).

The most persuasive argument that work is good is that God works. That man is to take his cue from God is first seen in God's resting on the seventh day, after working creatively for six. We know that God needs no rest, but He stopped His creative gesture at a point six days after beginning His work and thereafter commanded that man follow His pattern. As God worked and paused in His work, so man is told to work and break off in a pattern. With modern refinements, man returns to seven-day work cycles when he forgets that God ordained an alternation between work and rest. Modern man seems to have difficulty in coming to terms with the divine pattern. He ought to know that it is also the ideal human pattern.

Biblical Significance of Work

Before the fall of man, Adam was told to dress the garden and keep it. Work was thereby created under perfect conditions. When conditions changed, work continued, but in a different environment and with different motivation. Sweat of the human brow and physical weariness were joined by such enemies as weed and weather, weakness and wildness, blight and pest.

Woman's special work in bearing and nursing children is also a responsibility that relates to family work. A mother enters physical labor, sometimes with pain, to give birth. Beyond the bearing of children there is also the work of nurturing them.

The Genesis record teaches lessons of work and suggests the difficulty through which it is to be carried out. It is a natural warfare that must be fought, as man labors with, and sometimes against, nature.

Friend nature is also his foe. Rightly engaged, the natural war can be won. From our earliest knowledge of man, work has been known and accomplished with mixed success.

During the first century following the birth of Christ there were many jobs, even professions, for both free men and slaves. Some of the finest teachers were slaves who instructed their master's children, and sometimes their own. We know that Peter was a fisherman, Lydia sold cloth, and Paul and his friends Aquila and Priscilla were tentmakers. There were sailors, storekeepers, farmers. Barnabas accumulated and sold an estimable estate, turning the large proceeds over to the young church for distribution in relief. The ruins of ancient Pompeii, a city destroyed by the eruption of Vesuvius in the same period, reveal that there were well-to-do men and women among the common citizens of Rome. One extant painting from Pompeii is that of a fairly wealthy baker and his wife. Their place among the revelers of Pompeii was gained by the simple expedient of founding and running a successful business for profit twenty centuries ago.

A man, his wife and children in ancient times were committed to family work. Son generally followed father in a business or enterprise. Joseph, a carpenter, trained Jesus to be a carpenter. Apparently the family expected Jesus to succeed to a master's role in the craft. He chose rather to counsel, teach and preach; he became a rabbi, which in that ancient time was an honorable title bestowed on one whom the Jewish public felt deserving of honor. Work and occupation that provide family livelihood are as ancient as man's written history.

Work and Money

Barter systems preceded the invention of money, but later paralleled and supplemented money usage. Barter has never been totally lost, and it regains strength during inflationary times. Systems of exchange, although limited for common people, existed even in ancient civilizations. Biblical teachings about money, within the culture of those times, are cast in terms appropriate for current society. What the Bible has to say about money and business seems up to date.

During all written history there have been systems by which the production of a man could be translated into something negotiable. At first simple exchanges of goods or services were made, then valuable metals were weighed out in bulk to pay for a purchase. Coinage, beginning about 800 B.C., made business exchange easier.

By this money system business and family life became more easily organized, but changes were not as great as we might imagine. There was simply too little money in the hands of the masses. Even so exchange became easier. Taxes could be paid, trade between tribes could be carried on more rapidly, and wealth became a means for power, for expressing either evil or just intents.

The Scriptures everywhere imply that work is necessary for man, both for his purpose in the intelligent world and to his development in society. The lazy man is ordered to go to the ant, consider her ways and be wise. The ant is nothing if not a worker, a social insect, and a teacher of meaning for even human beings.

Man, if he is wise, makes work serve large and good ends. So he works.

Man, Woman and Work

The Scriptures appear to hold no real objection to the homogenizing process, when it is appropriate, for men and women in business and family, the thorough mixing of work that is direct (family services) and work that is indirect (salary to buy goods the family needs and wants). The writer of the closing chapter of Proverbs describes a wife/mother of superior competency in her home, in commerce, even in social charity. Her success is sufficiently large that her reputation is widespread in the community and brings related honor to her husband.

New Testament writers were not reluctant to refer to the success of such women as Lydia, who sold expensive purple cloth (Acts 16:14). Generally, the New Testament women are cast in contexts that highly commend them for the quality of their lives or sensitivity to spiritual truths. This is observed in the number of times a new church is born in the home or under the auspices of a woman or women. No criticism is advanced for Lydia, Priscilla, the daughters of Philip, or other specific women. Certainly, women like Jezebel and Athaliah are sometimes represented as evil persons, but women generally less so than men. Some observations about women, like the admonition in Philippians to Euodias and Syntyche, are modest. On balance, the New Testament, written in a male-dominated era in history, is dramatically radical in its teaching of equality for men and women (Gal. 3:28).

Business and Work

In developed countries a high rate of employment and satisfactory productivity from workers is needed for prosperity. Prosperity is unknown in cultures where the work ethic is absent. A *nation's well-being*, and sometimes survival, is directly related to the willingness of its people to work. Without work, the world with its large population would be unlivable and man would be unproductive. That part of the world with the least organized work and technology is the most ill-housed, ill-clothed, ill-fed. Life spans there are short and illness characterizes daily life.

Vital to the *well-being of any business* is the work done by its laborers. Work, when finished and measured, equals the rate of production for goods or services. There is at least a minimal level of production that must be maintained to cover the cost of labor if a business is to survive. Cost of labor is calculated as expensive or inexpensive in relation to worker efficiency. If costs exceed an acceptable level, the venture must be abandoned or funded in some special way. Many analysts believe any project that includes income and expense, except social services, should stand on its ability to support itself. If it cannot, this inability is generally taken as a sign that the project ought to be abandoned or dissolved. During some historical cycles, the cost of labor causes an industry to move from one state or province to another, even from one country to another. These and other dynamics in business life create excitement and challenge. On occasion too difficult to control they cost businesses their lives.

Some social studies suggest that work is necessary for achieving *personal well-being*. Persons who work are happier, healthier, and more competent to care for themselves than those who do not labor. Work is necessary to raise humanity above subsistence levels, to make life more dignified, and to give larger meaning to human existence. In short, there is a basic human need to work.

Most men, until this century, were farmers or closely related to rural enterprises. In modern times, in urban communities, the business world and family life depend on factory and office labor. If a man who is conditioned to work has taken responsibility for a family and then loses his job, he is a candidate for tragedy. A lost job is almost as serious in its emotional effects on a family as is the death of a loved one. The unemployed man or woman is shocked at the loss of his job. Self-esteem is threatened. Personal depression may follow, pessimism and anger rise as savings and alternatives are exhausted. Uncertainty, inertia, demoralization follow for some. Bitterness may take hold and never really abate. In a society that runs on a money system, the failure of jobs means the absence of money. There appears to be no other way to survive than get money. The most legitimate way to do so is work. Welfare, even when not abused, is an unsatisfactory alternative except as a temporary measure.

Human Work Needs

People need work for their own self-esteem. This is verified further in the experiences of physically and even mentally handicapped persons. Their work, perceived by them to be meaningful, settles their emotions and improves their concepts of themselves. Work is therapy for handicapped persons, men and women who could make excuse to escape labor. Persons with or without handicaps need the experience that work can give.

The human need to work may be depreciated by some individuals. This situation is partly caused by the failure of influential and vocal critics to recognize the importance of work for human fulfillment. Meaningful or worthwhile labor is sometimes ridiculed. Various arguments are advanced. They include the belief that hard-working people are too aggressive and warlike, that they are too exploitive, too materialistic. These are dangers, of course, but they can be met with controls. Such controls have to do with the laws limiting work schedules, with the nature of the products produced, with the education of the meaning and purposes of labor.

Work is sometimes criticized because it is not sufficiently creative. It takes time that could be invested in other matters such as literature, art and music. Response to such criticism is simply that there is ample time for all legitimate things. A balanced life finds respite from work and art.

A frequent objection to work in the machine age is that most jobs are monotonous, alleged to be dehumanizing. This must be true for some jobs, or becomes true if other motivations, such as love for family, are missing. But life is marked by repetitions, and when common jobs are enlarged and variety introduced, workers often rebel and request that duties be narrowed again. Man appears to hold love/hate relationships with his occupations. Contradictions about work are never resolved, but organized work continues to be a significant measure of man's advancement.

Family Work

In recent years social activists have denigrated work done solely for receiving money. Much of that denigration is simplistic, contributing little to understanding. But some critics have made helpful observations. One such writer is John Holt who has written about the differences between jobs, careers and work.

A "job," Holt says, is something you do for money, and only for money. A "career" is a "ladder of jobs" taking a person upward from one level to another. The higher he goes, the more interesting he finds it, the more authority he is given, the higher he is paid, and the less "hard-dirty-dangerous" are his assignments. "Work" Holt defines as "vocation" or "calling." By "calling" he means something that one would do for its own sake, something he would do for nothing (Holt 1980, 14).

The evangelical church has been among the last to give up calling as prime motivation for what one will do with his life. We regret that many, perhaps the majority of, Christian men and women have given up on calling and evaluate their worth by the amount of money they are paid. This attitude leads to loss of respect for job-work, what one does almost entirely for money. Money is not enough long-term motivation for life. Life worth spirals downward under those circumstances. Our lives are exchanged for official paper. Many analysts, for the most part secular, are themselves appalled with our preoccupation with money and materialism.

One cannot imagine that Jesus would go to speak at an

annual convention in Jerusalem for $2,000 per weekend. He
would not encourage men to fish for money, but to fish because they wanted to be fishermen and to provide food for
families hungry for fish. (The simple event of catching a
fish with a coin in his mouth by which He would pay
taxes has nothing to do with the principle discussed here.)
The test for calling is that I would do what I am doing if I
were paid nothing. I am not a hireling. This can be, and
must be, taught first by the family.

Goods and Services

Businesses are perceived as providing goods or services
desired by markets able to pay for what they get. Companies manufacturing beds, cars, shoes, furniture, and
other finished products provide goods. Companies offering
education, protection, cleaning, recreation, and main-
tenance programs provide services. Governments provide
services. Both goods and services, offered in sufficient
quality and quantity, represent the degree and nature of a
nation's economic and social development.

Families are also concerned with goods and services.
Traditionally, the husband/father was responsible to create or purchase from the proceeds of his labor most of the
goods needed by the family. The wife/mother provided the
majority of services and homemade products through
direct labor. In ideal balance, the work of husband and
wife were presumed to be complementary and sometimes
shared on special occasions, such as harvest time. With the
development of the technological age and the enlargement
of labor for wages, for work in business remote from the
laborer's home, new perceptions entered family considerations.

A man formerly cultivating potatoes began to work for
money to buy potatoes.

The shift from direct to indirect provision of goods was
not supposed to change the husband/father function. But it
did. The woman continued her services to the family, extending the former system. She did not, at first, partici-

pate in the transitional experience of her husband, receiving pay for work invested. At length, guided by the demands of world wars, many women entered the salaried labor force outside their homes. These social shifts appear to have affected the parenting role adversely.

The new perception holds that neither male nor female should be required to follow exclusively one or the other roles to deliver goods or services. It is commonly felt that human rights should be acknowledged and guaranteed so that the sex of a person should not prevent that person from becoming a wage earner. Better expressed, the sex of a person should not be the cause for advantage or disadvantage in the world of commerce. In the twentieth century, salaries and wages tilted the family away from an equation of goods and services and weighed matters in favor of goods. Women as well as men turned toward wages. With decline in respect for services, those in service industries demanded larger pay for their work. Through higher wages they could be recruited to perform the work.

Division of Labor

Accepting the equality concept for men and women, and for children as well, a family may utilize a philosophy of work that serves its needs and desires. Families need services like cooking, bed making, cleaning, garbage collecting, dishwashing, laundering—the list grows long. They also need food, houses, cars, clothes, furniture—this list also grows long. These services and goods may either be provided by the family or purchased by it.

If family members do all the chores, make their own clothes, cultivate their own garden, even make their own furniture, the family is self-provisioning. Only a small percentage of the needed goods and services are purchased. A lifestyle, wholly acceptable, if consistent, emerges from this self-contained family. In a world jammed with an immense population, that lifestyle is generally impractical. Percentages of self-contained families in advanced cultures decline year after year.

Other families choose another style. Members seek jobs paying salaries by which needs are met through purchases. They eat out often, they purchase everything they use, and they prefer to surrender some privileges of time together so that they may experience the luxury of the use of money. They have agreed on, or fall into, the pattern.

Those who adopt each lifestyle must remember that their choice of one pattern necessarily excludes some elements of the other. Failure to accept these differences is cause for considerable tension in pluralistic societies. Families selecting self-contained patterns cannot fairly or justly demand full privileges of money wealth. Those who choose to sell their time for wages in order to have purchasing power cannot expect to enjoy fully the casual life and personal freedom of those who opt for private interests and reduced affluence.

Choice of style of work and living can be illustrated in the business world. An acquaintance of mine successfully founded and developed a grocery store. His success was dramatic. Other stores in the city were made available to him. At last he was persuaded to expand. He lost nearly everything he had accumulated, but wisely divested himself of all but the first store before an inevitable tragedy would have destroyed him economically. He was a one-store man. His friendliness, attitudes, thought processes, real interests made him successful. His person and skills could not be extended beyond his home base. Another man, impersonal in a store, could succeed with a chain because of his skills for anticipating public buying tastes.

Nearly any style will serve a family if commitment to it is clear and generally accepted, and steps are taken to make it work. Whether the household chores are done by the women or divided with the men makes no difference if the members agree on the division of labor and make sure the work gets done. This is the crux of the matter—it must get done to general satisfaction. It is not there to be argued about, fought over, neglected. No style of life is satisfactory if the perceived work does not get done. Any style is acceptable if chores are done without rancor and the welfare of all members is properly considered. Any family style approved by the Christian community assumes the moral rightness of family life within the parameters of moral and social conduct. Biblical injunctions provide the boundary guidelines for that conduct. The Scriptures do not insist on some chores as women's work and others as men's work. They do insist on family peace.

Children and Labor

Two problems dominate family management as it relates to labor and children. The first is the nurture of children when both parents are occupied in the labor market outside the home. The second is the necessity for engaging children in meaningful work during their early years, as well as during adolescence. Both issues appear to be unresolved in many modern homes. Often adolescents are permitted to use gainful employment to substitute for formal schooling. The purchase of a car is made to be a substitute for earning a diploma. Or the imbalance may go the other way—school and leisure occupy the whole time of the high-schooler. It is the assumption here that there are several possibilities for solution, any combination of which might succeed for some families and fail for others. Readers of this book should well sense, by this time, that no one-and-only-one way of doing things is advocated. Again, effective management relates to the ability of managers to solve problems in the light of circumstances.

In these times, activists imply that women who devote themselves to domestic life are somehow enslaved or denied rights. It is well to reiterate that wives/mothers who wish to devote themselves to the care and keeping of home and family as the objectives of their workaday duties are making legitimate commitments. They find housekeeping, general home duties and child rearing significant ways to invest their lives. These are enhanced when, in addition, the women enlarge their lives with reading, arts, volunteer service and other opportunities for personal development. Most counselors discover that more women complain about their husbands "forcing" them to get jobs to help financially than complain because their husbands do not wish to have them work. Husbands are not in as much opposition to wives working as they are said to be.

The greatest advantage in the wife/mother-at-home pattern accrues to dependent children, especially for pre-school children. The older the children, the easier it is for them to adapt to an absentee mother or father (if the father is the major homemaker). Children need to be parented, or nurtured, and some satisfactory arrangement must be made.

If mother and father must be absent from home at the same time, there is no reason why a parent figure—grandparent, elder child (if old enough, and responsible enough), or someone else—cannot serve in appropriate ways. When substitutes are made, the actual parents, the most authoritative persons in a child's life, make up for their absence by improving the quality of intimacy with their children when opportunities for contact are afforded. They share family objectives, gain agreement for participation from the children in family goals, and create rewarding situations, recognized as such by the children. For example, many farm children agree on the crops and herds to be raised on the family property. They are partly rewarded by owning one of the animals and sharing in the bounty of the harvest.

When each member is required to participate in the work of the family, the family becomes a unit and is drawn into a loyal circle. This is the reason why some families succeed even when both parents develop outside careers. Managing time is vital so that when unusual professional demands are made on one mate the other can be free to be with the children. Doing chores together is another way to win family success. Enjoying the work is necessary accompaniment to the effort.

Respect for work, proper attitudes while engaged in it, and appropriate rewards for it are all part of effective and enlightened management in either business or family. These factors are added to others for the purpose of developing a program of family "labor relations."

Reading about Work and the Family

Authors with Christian or generally Christian emphases:

Berry, Jo. *The Happy Home Handbook.* Old Tappan, N.J.:
Revell, 1976. (pp. 41-80.)
Johnson, James. *The Nine-to-Five Complex.* Grand Rapids:
Zondervan, 1972.
Lee, Mark W. *How to Have a Good Marriage.* Chappaqua,
N.Y.: Christian Herald, 1978. ("What is your attitude
about your wife's working outside the home?" pp. 98-
102; "What is your attitude toward household chores?"
pp. 150-52.)
Petersen, J. Allan. *For Men Only.* Wheaton, Ill.: Tyndale,
1973. (Chap. 4, pp. 117-42.)
Schaeffer, Edith. *Hidden Art.* Wheaton, Ill.: Tyndale, 1971.

Authors with secular or generally secular emphases:

Bolles, Richard Nelson. *What Color Is Your Parachute?*
Berkeley, Calif.: Ten Speed Press, 1972 and later
editions.
Gagnon, John H. and Cathy S. Greenblat. *Life Designs.*
Palo Alto, Calif.: Scott, Foresman, 1978. (pp. 341-407.)
Holt, John. *Growing Without Schooling.* New York:
Delacorte Press, 1980.

CHAPTER 12

Finances

● **How does a business administer its finances?**

● **How does a family plan the use of its resources?**

Owe no man any thing, but to love one another (Rom. 13:8).

For the children ought not to lay up for the parents, but the parents for the children (2 Cor. 12:14).

Charge them that are rich in this world, that they be not highminded, nor trust in uncertain riches, but in the living God, who giveth us richly all things to enjoy: That they do good, that they be rich in good works, ready to distribute, willing to communicate; Laying up in store for themselves a good foundation against the time to come, that they may lay hold on eternal life (1 Tim. 6:17-19).

The biblical view of wealth—of persons, or families, or churches, or governments or businesses—relates to spiritual and social responsibility. Wealth is a problem, according to the Scriptures, when it is used selfishly or taken as a substitute god. Unsurrendered affection, for money or anything else, is unacceptable for Christian life and development. Wealth causes concern even for the rich man, who feels that many other human beings, even those critical of wealth, are trying to get what he has. If that wealth is so attractive to the poor, why should it not be attractive to the rich? Why is wealth so important?

The Bible and Wealth

As noted earlier, the ancient Jews commonly related prosperity to God's blessing. If God blessed Israel there would be plenty, and if the glory of God departed there would be poverty. When Israel was at the height of her spiritual life, under Solomon, a major evidence of that development was economic success. The Queen of Sheba so interpreted the status and life of Solomon and Israel (1 Kings 10:2-7). The Scriptures everywhere imply the connection.

The Temple of Solomon was opulent. The use of gold, the best woods, the accoutrements, and the vessels of worship were taken as matter of course. Solomon's house rivaled any palace of the time in that part of the world. In modern times we may have difficulty in relating the simple Christian lifestyle with the grandeur of Solomon's.

When Israel and Judah went into spiritual decline, both wealth and prowess were lost for the kings and people. The key perception in analyzing the cycles of wealth and poverty in the Bible is that, for God's people, wealth stems from respect for God and practice of good stewardship. For Israel the status of stewardship was partly disclosed in the mission of tithes.

Wealth might be gained through effective business practices, or even chicanery, but for the spiritual person and family, wealth is supposed to flow out of obedience to God and is achieved through the stewardship of resources. Because wealth is only one of the evidences of God's blessing, and because only some of God's children are themselves provided that evidence, the Christian with much is instructed to be generous (1 Tim. 6:17-19). Other evidences and gifts than wealth are provided to most believers.

The concern of a Christian family is that all it has should be perceived initially as God's provision rather than the return of the exercise of superior intellect, management, or cleverness on the part of the elders in the family. But acknowledging first cause does not displace subsidiary causes. Provided the gift of material resources, the family managers ought to use them with care. This care or practice of excellent planning is, in itself, proof of the application of family management for its material wealth. In a sense biblical stewardship is a means of worship. Without stewardship our blessings may be dissipated.

To keep money or wealth in balance with other factors and use it in acceptable ways, one must plan stewardship. Basic patterns are fairly clear for any plan. Without planning there is likely to emerge inferior stewardship for us.

The Profit Motive in Business

Most businesses follow a simple purpose: to make a profit by providing goods or services needed by a public. Ostensibly, this is done in an ethical context. From the Christian point of view, business contexts ought to be ethical in every situation. That standard means more than avoidance of wrongdoing. It is a positive effort to better the lot of individuals and society through business processes.

This statement of general business purpose—to derive an ethical procedure in providing for human wants and needs through corporate means, making a reasonable profit—is itself simple, but achievement is more difficult than words imply. Planning, with all it entails, should be included in a business. Owners or managers dare not leave matters to chance. Someone in authority should have an idea about where the business is headed, how much it will cost to get there, how expenses will be met, and how much will be left over when accounts have been balanced.

All fiscal planning is guided by a philosophy of management that includes control of cash flow, borrowing, investment return, depreciation, profits and other factors. For example, a company generally expects to realize 5 to 10 percent as a profit return on its capital investment.

Many businesses make more—much more; many less—
much less. If a million dollars is invested, the manager
might well be disappointed if he cannot show at least
$60,000 profit at the end of the year. If he cannot, it would
have been better financially for him *not* to have established the company. He might have done well to sell out
and bank the sale price. Bank interest would provide at
least as much profit to him without high risk, exacting
labor, or personal concern.

There are, of course, other factors that affect the decision to continue in business. Without those factors, motivation would not be great enough for some people to establish businesses. I have known farmers who have invested more than a half million dollars in land and
machinery. Some years they lose money. In others they
make a profit, sometimes a handsome one, but it is doubtful that many average as much as 2 percent profit on their
investment. Most persons would not be willing to work for
that return. Selling out, they could invest what they
receive and find some other occupation to follow. But those
men are farmers: they love the soil, the air, the animals,
the independence, the way of life.

There are more values than profit included in the
formulas some persons design for their business lives.
Nevertheless, one cannot follow even his most favored activity if the financial drain in doing so is too great. He
cannot take losses indefinitely. He must include funding
among factors important to him.

Although business survival and growth are dependent on
profit, that motive is not without its critics. Criticism is
understandable when the profit motive is controlled by
greed, pride and irresponsibility. For some people dis-
illusionment with capitalism is great, partly because of unethical practices of profit fanatics. An economy using
profit as the only test of its success is not only unworthy
of defense, critics argue, but ought to sink into oblivion or
be destroyed. Such a view is ardently held by anticapita-
list radicals. Radicals argue that the old must be de-

stroyed before a new and better system can be introduced
and be expected to succeed. Radicals do not repair systems. They can work only with their own perceptions.

One of the basic problems in any economic theory—capitalism, socialism, communism, or even barterism—is that
none has ever been able to overcome human greed and
other negative factors in man's character, factors that
generate evil or unsocial conduct. Any social theory a community *wills* to succeed may be expected to work as well
as any other. Theory is not likely the evil in the economic
or historical piece. Men and women easily distort ideals in
any theory. The evil is in men, not in theories, except that
men devise imperfect theories.

Capitalism is the favored theory in the Western world
because, as commonly believed, it provides with some efficiency the most goods and services for the greatest
number of citizens by utilizing the profit motive. Problems
of pernicious greed and lack of self-control force government intervention into business and personal life. By inter-
vening, government hopes to safeguard ethics. Its record of
accomplishment is uneven. The tug-of-war between manufacturer and consumer, between government and business,
has never been settled. Good and evil appear in the
watchers and the watched. But this issue of ethics will appear in the closing chapter of this writing.

Businesses are concerned with budgets, contingencies,
plant funds, depreciation, cash flow, reserves, benefits and
controls. We find all of these in family business. Like businesses, families may prosper or go bankrupt.

Family Resources and Planning

Perhaps the larger issues of business and government
may be observed in miniature through family fiscal activity. Even the watcher and watched appear in family money
management. The spender, the bill payer, the controller of
family funds is the mate watched, with the remaining mate
and sometimes the children serving as watchers. These
roles, related to money management, are sometimes con-

sciously and sometimes unconsciously perceived by one or both mates as master and servant roles. One serves as management, and the other as labor or consumer protectionist. Each sometimes presumes the other to be unfair, misunderstanding and even incompetent. A wife, in requesting funds or information from her husband, may feel she is denigrated. He feels he is watched and doubted. The tension is not unlike that which occurs between labor unions and industrial management, or even between managers at various levels in the same company.

Is a family concerned with profits? Another question almost leaps out to imply an answer: Why not? A family ought to be concerned, at the least, to take in a bit more than it spends. This does not mean that money is the dominant, overriding, obsessive concern of a family, but there ought to be sensible management that tries to keep family costs within the boundaries of its income. And part of the sense of well-being in a family may relate to its ability to increase its capital worth. This incorporates some of the meaning of the apostle's recollection that parents lay up for their children (2 Cor. 12:14).

Perhaps the best philosophy of money is that it is a *tool*. As some artisans are more skillful than others with their tools, so some persons are more effective than others in utilization of money. I have found that about half of my counselees admit they do not handle family funds well. More men than women say they are poor at budget control. In a family of ten members, adults and children, nearly half will manage money moderately well and half will not. With some training, all members could improve, although some will continue to demonstrate superiority. Adequate instruction about money management given early to children greatly enhances their chances for later success in balancing their income and outgo to accomplish personal goals.

Money as a tool is a means by which appropriate expectations are built into realities. One generally has an idea about what he wishes to accomplish. He may need many things to gain anticipated ends. He may need supporting people, education, blocks of time, opportunity—among other factors. In addition, he needs food, shelter, clothing, transportation and security. Nearly all factors are related to skillful investment of resources, including money.

Money is paper, but it is paper with vested values. It is legal return for human labor. It is a means of transfer of my labor or goods for another's. To understand that fact and use it for the care and benefit of a family is a matter of knowledge, wisdom and self-control. Money is to be controlled, not to be controlling. It is a means, not an end. Money is the wire that transfers resources from the generator to the receiver.

Planning

Plans reduce the potential number of errors. They speed up activity, once activity is begun. By planning, an individual maps the direction he wishes to take. Those sharing his experience are informed about anticipated courses of events. They are afforded an early review, being called on to respond to proposals and offer amendments. Once agreed upon, a specific plan becomes the shared project of all persons involved. They become committed to it as part of their own objectives and feel obligated to make it succeed. They are less likely to sabotage a known program they helped form than an unknown one imposed on them.

If feasible a couple should work out, during early months of betrothal and marriage, objectives for life, at least for employment years. This will include job, children, education, home, even vacations. And it means planning in advance for expenses, for investments, for wills (including the care of dependent children), and ultimately, retirement. Drawing up models or charts of what a couple wishes to accomplish, with a timetable, is great fun. The charts may be amended at any time feelings or circumstances change for the couple.

At least once or twice yearly, either at income tax time or at the conclusion of a calendar year, a "fiscal checkup" should be made. Interim evaluations on a quarterly basis will provide an early warning system of possible difficulties. Appropriate questions include: Are our wills in satisfactory order, or should they be updated? Should we shift our financial plan in any way? Is this a good year to have a special project? (Some adventurous families move for six months or a year to another country in order to enjoy a special experience.) Should we change our savings program in any way? Should we change banks? Must we shift our plans to meet educational expenses for our children? Do we need to establish a larger retirement plan? Do we need more insurance coverage for ourselves or our property? Do we have the right attitude toward money? Are we giving away a fair share of our earnings?

Necessities, Reserves, Luxuries

The beginning of planning is to project family necessities, reserves and luxuries—in that order. There should be some of each in every good plan. If any one is omitted, it is likely a poor plan, needing revision or overhaul. Or the family situation may have to be changed. For example, the wage earner, to do what he believes he ought to do, may need to look for a different job from the one he holds at the moment. He feels that he must have more money. Or he may get along with less. He wishes to do some good things unrelated to money making. He should measure the factors carefully.

Necessities are food, shelter, transportation, clothing, taxes, education, and giving. A family should eat wholesome diets, should live in a home large enough to accommodate the personal needs of members, should transport members to and from home, work, school or store. Members should be dressed suitably for work and worship. All should contribute money, assisting others who are in need, unless they are the ones requiring that assistance.

Reserves are savings for emergencies and money for specials like vacation periods, general security preparatory to retirement, and the like. These provide a sense of well-being. Savings, life insurance, and real estate may be included in this plan for reserves. A couple saving $50 monthly for forty years will likely have a nest egg at retirement of more than $250,000. Depending on investments, it could be more. Depending on emergencies, it could be less. In retirement one might draw a handsome monthly check, drawing upon both interest and capital, for many years. It is likely that some residue would remain at the time of death. If savings are made early and remain untouched, the interest earnings, compounded, create dramatic accumulations.

If life insurance is purchased early in life, the annual cost of premiums is lower, and the length of protection is longer. Traditionally, the largest volume of insurance is carried on the wage earner. There are various insurance plans to meet family needs. The wise planner buys neither too much nor too little insurance.

If a home or condominium is purchased—a structure expected to improve in value because of its location or because material and labor invested by the owners increase its value—the family may be accumulating potential income on its own living quarters. Or a duplex purchased may meet two interests: a place to live and the means to pay, at least partially, for both units.

Luxuries refer to some types of vacations or recreation, personal property like jewelry, hobbies and special projects. Some kinds of clothing, or equipment, or gourmet foods are luxuries. What is *not* necessary to daily life or for future projections may be thought of as luxury. Modest desire for luxury is healthy. On occasion the luxuriating experience provides a healing effect.

Methods

The success secret in money management, in a *small* business as in a family, is to figure income on a conservative basis, and never permit expenditures to exceed income. There are basic economic principles that cannot be set aside if families or businesses are to flourish. Mr. Micawber, the friend of David Copperfield, put the issue well for a family when he advised his young counselee:

> My other piece of advice, Copperfield, . . . you know. Annual income twenty pounds, annual expenditure nineteen six, result happiness. Annual income twenty pounds, annual expenditure twenty pounds ought and six, result misery. The blossom is blighted, the leaf is withered, the God of day goes down upon the dreary scene and—in short you are for ever floored. As I am! (Dickens, chap. 12).

For the young family, conservative planning includes only the basic take-home pay for one wage earner. This leaves the family financially able to include children. All necessities should be met from the single salary. And this plan does not include tax refunds, bonuses or gifts. Commonly, such special income matches unforeseen emergencies.

Life should be as debt free as possible. One should anticipate and save for future expenditures. Such saving is aided by interest accumulations on reserves. Savings for emergencies should be placed in high-yielding bank notes, certificates or accounts. Week-by-week shifts change investment opportunities and priorities. Treasury bills sometimes draw twice the income interest that a standard savings account may provide. Interest accumulation increases income without requiring personal work beyond that which earned the original capital.

Markets, credit, worth, investment, risk, interest and collateral are words that, in finance, were once used almost exclusively by bankers and financiers. Currently, they are common to millions of citizens who own a few shares of stock in IBM, or General Motors, or Quaker Oats, or some utility, or any one of thousands of stock and bond securities available for purchase. Most citizens remain naive in the complications of "float," or "margin," or "futures."

Perhaps that ignorance is beneficial for the most part, for them and for society. They might play too much without adequate knowledge to accomplish the purpose of economic risk. Unless a person holds some expertise and is more than ordinarily affluent, he should avoid significant investment in the stock or other fluctuating markets. Market investments entail risk of capital. Many persons cannot afford that risk. And some do not have heart for it even if they are wealthy enough to invest.

By delay in purchasing anything, the individual maintains interest accumulations on the savings he would have invaded to make purchases. Delay may be possible because an appliance or product is not really necessary at the time. Or repairs may be made economically on equipment in service. Once the desire to have something new and have it immediately has moderated, the cost of living drops for a family, sometimes dramatically. Acquisitiveness is a disease which, if not cured, requires attenuation of some sort. Delay is often useful for weakening buying urges. Even large companies compel delays through policies to assure that outlays are really needed. Buy it later.

Cutting expenses is an excellent way to "increase" income. Renting an apartment for $100 a month less than is currently being paid is equivalent to a raise of $100 a month made available for other things. Lifestyle changes, to more or less luxury, account for dramatic changes in living expenses and available income.

A person must decide on his own primary values in ownership. Believing that there is little valuable collateral in anything except land and home, one may reduce desire for acquisition of other property. Everything else may be seen as "junk." Cars, appliances, clothes, furniture, and the like have little value except to the owner of them. They are tools that respond to a service-oriented, comfortable life. They are not worth much in the money market. In a few years they will be worn out, or sent to a junk dealer, or carried to the community dump.

Keeping fantasies and wishes within the limits of an

income can be a pleasant experience as a couple makes a game of money planning. Games have limits—there are only so many pieces to play with, out-of-bounds markers are clear, impediments slow progress to victory—but all are a part of the game, giving it mystery and romance. To stay within the boundaries of known resources means the game will be a pleasant experience. Chances of winning are high. Risks are reduced. The rules are designed by the players in the budget game. These are the things we will do, these we want to do if we can, and these we will not do. The players begin. Everyone can win—if he keeps the rules.

Inflation Games

It is likely that money viewpoints change for families as they do for business. When they do, money management shifts direction. For example, inflation is perceived by one family as dangerous. The family moves into action. Precautions must be taken, the family believes, to guard against inflation by cutting back expenditures, reducing lifestyle, buying fewer luxuries or nonessentials. The family decides to postpone purchases, or even sell property while prices are relatively high, and hold tight until the economy shifts and money becomes more valuable. Their self-denial is an accepted risk. One loses some of his goals in this conservation if he does not outlive inflation. He must live long enough for the cycle to break. For example, if he waits for the cost of housing to drop before buying a home and prices do not drop, he may never own a home.

A second couple, with similar income and assets as the first, interprets inflation differently. Inflation, they believe, will continue indefinitely so that buying now is cheaper than buying later. This family may presume to take advantage of its rich credit rating and buy more than it would under other circumstances. This policy actually stimulates inflation, but that is what the couple is planning for anyway. A house may be purchased at a high price for speculation to be sold a year or two later at an even higher price for profit. Art objects or "collectables" are treated similarly.

Those who take the "new inflation outlook" take risks, but they presume they have a right to do so. Many have reaped personal benefit as inflation escalated. They entered an economic pattern at a juncture when the spiral was moving upward and continued to do so. They played out the game, to win or lose. The risk is that the spiral will start down before profits are taken, or before payments are completed. As long as prices rise the inflation player will appear to be a successful money-manager, even money-maker. Those players caught in the shift downward are the ones who will be hurt economically.

A person who manages his affairs after an experience of financial depression tends to look on inflation as an evil and those who fuel it to be foolish, perhaps unethical. The younger inflationist perceives money in a different way entirely. That a dollar means a quarter in comparison with a dollar twenty years earlier means nothing to him. Relative percentages become more vital to his experience. If costs rise 10 percent while his salary rises 12, he is little concerned with the monetary values of his father's day. He feels he is better off. At least for this moment, he is.

Because millions of wage earners have, through labor contracts or company policies, gained regular cost-of-living increases (this is known as indexing, itself an impressive inflationary influence), inflation is often viewed by these workers as beneficial for their families. However, they may be ambivalent in public responses they make to inflation. Established, older, well-managed families are not nearly as affected by inflation as are new families. Home paid for, or mortgage set, automobile owned, children's education complete, or nearly so, a family does not experience cost increases equal to its wage increases.

On the other hand, cost of living for newlyweds is greater, sometimes much greater, than the rate of economic escalation might imply. Young couples cannot hope to reside in some cities unless circumstances substantially

change. They have too few resources to purchase, or even
rent, housing. They cannot afford the cost of urban living.
But their circumstances cannot be selectively improved.
Labor demands across-the-board wage raises.

Youthful members of society have been resourceful none-
theless. Revolutionary youth in the 1960s loudly com-
plained against materialism and the values of their elders.
That collegiate generation became, in fact, practicing ma-
terialists. They purchased houses, cars, services, and recre-
ational equipment at a younger age and in greater quantity
than their parents. Much of it was put "on the tab." Rules
were liberalized. For example, a new auto could be paid for
in twenty-four or thirty months after World War II. By the
1950s, three-year loans became common. Four years
became standard in the 1970s. As a part of the same shift
in viewpoint, a house was mortgaged with only one income
in the formula during the decade of the 1950s. By the late
1970s, both husband's and wife's incomes could be lumped
into the formula. A mortgage of $60,000 was easier to get
during inflationary 1979 than one of $20,000 in 1959. The
new dynamics, accepted by youths, frightened many of
their elders.

But in 1980 there was a general shift to some former
practices, and some funding ceased. Businessmen and
government absorbed available bank capital for commerce at high interest rates. Easy credit was shut off. Even
fees were charged for personal credit cards. Qualifications
for personal or family loans became more stringent. Cost of
borrowed money went up to all-time records, then alternately rose and fell. Accurate predictions about what one
might be able to do were more and more difficult to make.
Even well-known analysts argued that effective future
planning for families or industry was less probable than
earlier. Authors published new books on business based on
new theories.

The complexities of money management make it impossible to affirm with confidence exactly how each family
will or ought to function. As some nations and some insti-

tutions will not survive without judicious use of credit, some families feel they too should use credit to advance their interests and ultimate fortunes. In the end, justification of what is done must be based on many factors. It is the responsibility of each family to know those factors and weigh them. *Weigh* them, not count them.

Weighing Factors

Objectives enter as a primary consideration. If a major objective of family members is to remain debt free in every part of their lives, money management might be different from that of a couple entering a business venture. The second family may succeed by incurring debt, whereas they would miss their special goals if they held the debt-free objective of the first couple. Debt incurrence, in any case, ought to relate to sufficient collateral to guarantee loans.

Some money goals are dramatic, but many are made by people who do not weigh the consequences of their plans. Sometimes couples set objectives, let us say, for earning half a million dollars by the time the husband reaches a particular birthday. In a striking number of instances, they achieve or nearly achieve their goals. Some are happy with their success. But some clearly are not and ultimately request counseling. Although they have achieved their financial goals, the human cost has been too great. Because they have worked so hard at their business, their family life has suffered: they lost the intimacy of their marriage relationship, their interests became more materialistic and less personal and spiritual. Their children were neglected and partly alienated. They had little social life. They found that wealth does not bring happiness, but in many cases they still do not want to release the security that it gives them. They appear to be caught in a web, a web they spun.

An important issue relates to the personality and tolerance levels of the husband and wife. If either is fearful about risk, is troubled when investments or events appear imperfect, feels amateurish about "high finance," and the

like, there ought to be strict limitation on anything but
standard, easily agreed-on conduct. The standard would be
to distribute income for necessities, giving, savings and
recreation by a carefully designed formula that the family
accepts.

Each personality must weigh factors on the basis of economic possibilities that he himself can manage safely and
well. Each needs to weigh the costs of time, relationships,
ideals, tolerances, goals, in determining how he will view
the rewards related to money.

Reading Related to Finances

Authors with Christian or generally Christian emphases:

Hardisty, George and Margaret. *Successful Financial Planning*. Old Tappan, N.J.: Revell, 1978.

Hastings, Robert J. *My Money and God*. Nashville: Broadman, 1961.

Lee, Mark W. *Creative Christian Marriage*. Glendale, Calif.: Regal, 1977. (Chap. 10-11, pp. 145-59.)

_____. *How to Have a Good Marriage*. Chappaqua, N.Y.: Christian Herald, 1978. ("Do you believe anyone should help you financially?" pp. 102-04; "What is your plan for budgeting?" pp. 107-10; "Who will balance the checkbook?" pp. 110-12; "Have you discussed giving to worthy causes?" pp. 112-14; "What is your attitude toward debt?" pp. 114-16.)

Petersen, J. Allan. *For Men Only*. Wheaton Ill.: Tyndale, 1973. (Chap. 5, pp. 143-74.)

Authors with secular or generally secular emphases:

Goldberg, Herb and Robert T. Lewis. *Money Madness*. New York: William Morrow, 1978.

Hallman, G. Victor and Jerry S. Rosenbloom. *Personal Financial Planning*. 2nd ed. San Francisco: McGraw-Hill, 1978.

Urus, Auren. *Over 50*. Radnor, Pa.: Chilton Book Co., 1979.

Section Five
PHILOSOPHY

CHAPTER 13 • *Ethics*

An important part of a complete philosophy of life is a theory of ethics. Ethics includes a concern with right and wrong in individuals and one's own culture, and for Christians, shadings of differences between absolute good and absolute evil. The Scriptures present a theory of ethics for man, and how standards may be kept or broken. Business practices commonly reflect human willingness to keep or break value systems. Whatever business does affects workers, customers, and society in general. Like business corporations and other institutions, a family is greatly affected by its own theory and practice of ethics. For nearly all persons, the issues of life are decided through value systems. Values are foundational and building happiness for himself and solidarity for his family.

CHAPTER **13**

Ethics

- **What is appropriate conduct for a business?**

- **What is appropriate conduct for a family?**

Therefore all things whatsoever ye would that men should do to you, do ye even so to them: for this is the law and the prophets (Matt. 7:12).

The soul that sinneth, it shall die. The son shall not bear the iniquity of the father, neither shall the father bear the iniquity of the son: the righteousness of the righteous shall be upon him, and the wickedness of the wicked shall be upon him (Ezek. 18:20).

Thou shalt not bow down thyself to them, nor serve them: for I the Lord thy God am a jealous God, visiting the iniquity of the fathers upon the children unto the third and fourth generation of them that hate me (Exod. 20:5).

The primary purpose of the Bible is to unfold the story of salvation. That story begins with the first human couple, proceeds through the dramatic religious history of tribal Israel (the spiritual microcosm and analogy of all peoples), to the life, death, resurrection and ascension of Jesus, and the breakaway of the Church for the purpose of Christian evangelism and nurture in the world, among all men, women and children. According to the Bible, this is to continue until the end of the age, at which time will occur the spiritual and literal recovery of the creation in righteousness through Christ, under God, the Father.

Biblical Standards of Ethics

A purpose of the Scriptures is to provide an ethical system by which mankind can survive and flourish even in a world where evil, tragedy and death stalk all living things. The ethical standards of Scripture inform us about many issues, including the nature of God and the nature of man. Also included in the narrative are the promises of reward for keeping these standards and punishment for breaking them. Righteousness is a key factor in determining standards. Applied righteousness is an attitude and pattern of human conduct that approaches the standards of a holy God.

Among the most dramatic warnings about violation of righteousness is that the human results of violation may extend through several family generations. There is a corporate family and social meaning to what is done by an individual. What he does, for good or ill, affects his family, both currently and in the future. The individual and the group are intertwined. I cannot deny either my identity as a person, or my corporateness as part of a group. The most simple application of the dual roles is my daily life as an individual and as a family member.

The Scriptures relate the conduct of parents and children to leadership quality in spiritual life (1 Tim. 3:4-5). This test of family effectiveness is stated straightforwardly: *Let deacons be husbands of only one wife, and good managers of their children and their own households* (1 Tim. 3:12, NASB). If one is effective in his family he may, thereby, reveal potential for larger assignment. If he fails in the smaller but vital relationship, he may easily be expected to fail in the larger privilege in the church. This is not necessarily the way things will happen, and he may not fail, but the evidence implies its own direction. And we tend to go by implication.

Biblical Corporate Ethics

The principle that failures of forefathers are visited upon their sons is not easy to accept, especially in a time when nearly every family must bear concern for at least one member violating corporate standards. It is likely that the biblical injunction is interpreted as one-sided and too severe. The *iniquity of the fathers* is visited upon the third and fourth generations of *those who hate me* (Exod. 20:5). The passage might well mean that consequences of iniquity continue for those generations making no affirmative change in their conduct. There is reason to believe, as time elapses, that people get tired of any increased burden of depravity. After declining decades, society turns around again, at least in part. To reinforce through several generations the evil of the first might influence change for good in the conduct of an ensuing generation. Even if it does not, God's jealousy for perfection appears to abate and the mercy of God lightens the load of later generations emerging from the shadows of their forefathers' acts. The mercy and love of God are that extensive.

The other side of the coin is that God shows loving-kindness to those who follow in the train of righteous forefathers. There is residual effect for good as there is for bad. If ensuing generations from this one fall into decline, they too exhaust those residual benefits from their ancestry. The point is made that one generally influences his posterity for good or ill, and for significant periods of time. It behooves him to act in ethical fashion to benefit his children, their children, and generations beyond his life span.

If anyone will follow the route of grace and forgiveness, he will not be continuously held by a negative pull of moral heredity. Ezekiel explains that the individual may, by his own choice, shift either the threat or the benefit by his own actions (Ezek. 18:14-32). Repentance assures the individual or the group that iniquity will not become an ever-present stumbling block. It is a larger barrier if it is permitted to build through generations. The prophet argues: *Therefore, repent and live* (Ezek. 18:32). The generational threat can be effectively put down.

Various biblical families enlarge for us an understanding of the momentum for good or evil through several generations. King David's sons were sometimes violent and proud, a negative reflection on their father, and perhaps mother. Haggith, mother of Adonijah, seems to have exerted some negative effect on him. But David must carry the largest responsibility. We know David failed his children by his permissiveness (1 Kings 1:5). He sought a release from his own guilt through repentance. Bath-sheba seems to have done well by her son Solomon. David's influence for good (humble repentance) followed beneficially through Solomon's line. David was given a covenant promise of perpetuity for his bloodline. That David's reliance on God, demonstrated by sorrow for sin and ensuing repentance, achieved benefits of divine grace for generations, is asserted by the writer of First Kings: *Abijam became king over Judah. . . . And he walked in all the sins of his father . . . and his heart was not wholly devoted to the Lord his God. . . . But for David's sake the Lord his God gave him a lamp in Jerusalem, to raise up his son after him and to establish Jerusalem: because David did what was right in the sight of the Lord* (1 Kings 15:1-5).

From Jeroboam, the first king of the northern kingdom following Solomon's death, we find the trace of evil through generations to the end of Jeroboam's bloodline. Jeroboam ruled over Israel, followed by his son Nadab. Baasha, a warrior, defeated Nadab, killing him and all issue stemming from Jeroboam—*because of the sins of Jeroboam which he sinned, and which he made Israel sin* (1 Kings 15:30). But Baasha also *walked in the way of Jeroboam* (1 Kings 15:34). Then the descendants from Baasha were struck down because of the sins of Baasha (1 Kings 16:12-13). Ensuing stories repeat the litany.

What the relevant Scriptures argue for, explain and il-
lustrate is the social corporate ethic. This ethic is easiest
to follow in the smallest institution, the family, where
there is greater simplicity than is found in larger corporate units. When the corporate family ethic is applicable, as
we noted earlier, the father bears greatest responsibility in
a self-giving example (loving), the wife follows that love
with a cooperative spirit (submission), and the child is
subordinate (obedient) to both parents. Ideally, each
person is rewarded for corporate participation, and each
takes primary responsibility commensurate with each suggested role. Each member assists the others in life course,
taking obligations of love, submission and obedience as
events suggest alignments among family members.

The greatest corporate ethical responsibility, as suggested above, rests on the husband/father, because love precedes either submission or obedience, and affords them ap-
propriateness. Love was first in God's motives relating to
man. Given the nature of God as perfect and loving, the
only sensible response by mankind is submission and
obedience. Imperfect as it is, the family attempts to follow
the divine order to achieve human corporate order. Love,
submission and obedience are far more important for
society and the family than we have imagined.

In reviewing the duties of citizens to government,
Romans 13 makes an application of corporate social ethics.
Leaders of government, states the Apostle Paul, will be
held responsible for the actions of nations they lead. If
they lead men to war, they must bear the ethical responsibility for what the soldier does, when the soldier possesses
no authority over his own life and activity. Leaders are responsible for the people they lead, when those they lead
are submissive and obedient to laws. When there is a
leader and a person led, there is context for corporate
ethics.

Certainly there are many issues related to ethics. Biblical commandments relate to personal morality—truth-
telling, sexual purity and fidelity, spiritual integrity, and

other moral matters. As important as these are, we pass over them, assuming their treatment elsewhere. Our concern here is with corporate perception, the damping of some individual freedoms and rights to protect and nurture an intimate group known as the family. In the biblical concept of the family this concern for others is a leading ethical matter related to Christian obedience to God. Widespread disregard among many Christians for family servanthood and solidarity shows, at best, ignorance of the biblical ethical standard for a family, particularly the Christian family.

Business Ethics and the Family

Ethics is sometimes called the "science of morals." By science we understand orderly approaches to a field of study—in this case, right and wrong. What is better than what we are doing? What is best? As suggested earlier, not all business theories incorporate extensive reviews of ethics. Some theorists merely assume that businesses will keep the laws of the land, and that is the extent of the matter. Our assumption here is that lawkeeping alone as an ethical standard is insufficient to both the best business practices as well as unsatisfactory for the business to family analogy appearing throughout this writing.

In discussing the business practices common to Japanese corporations, Pascale and Athos are forced to return often to the word *spiritual*. They are ready to admit that the spiritual and family concepts for business are likely to be seen as foreign to the aggressive "macho" approach pertaining to much of the theory and practice of American or Western managers. But they insist on superiority, proved in the marketplace, for the base of spiritual and family conceptions of business. Pascale and Athos call this base "superordinate goals" and they place it at the center of their management model. It is their managerial molecule (Pascale and Athos 1981, 326). They further relate a general decline of life quality in America to the loss of values, the loss or weakening of superordinate goals (Pascale and Athos 1981, 319). Nations, businesses, families, persons should hold and utilize those values and faith. So argue these business professors.

Perhaps the loss of respect for the business world by the general public is due to the felt loss of human and spiritual values in many corporations. Pascale and Athos found that the best corporations, some of which were gigantic, have not lost their beliefs, beliefs that have religious, even evangelistic, flavor. Key to business success, for business in general, is the recovery of this basic ethical position. They write:

> By an accident of history, we in the West have evolved a culture that separates man's spiritual life from his institutional life. . . .

> We recognize that some readers will resist the specter of a merger between "the Church and the corporation." But that is not what we are proposing. There is an important difference between religiosity and spirituality (Pascale and Athos 1981, 309-11).

More corporations should see their cultural responsibility "to respond truly to inner meanings that many people seek in their work—or alternately, seek in their lives and could find at work if only that were more culturally acceptable" (Pascale and Athos 1981, 311). Employers should not leave the employee to "fend for himself in adversity and draw upon the problematic spiritual resources available to him from friends, family and religious affiliations" (Pascale and Athos 1981, 311). Such companies as ServiceMaster, numerous publishing firms, even IBM, in America either maintain, or at one time did include, value orientation that is not only good for the employee, the customer, and their families, but good for business. Loss of that perception and practice can be destructive, even catastrophic, for business.

The whole matter affects business ethics. When there is

a spiritual perception, there is also a view of right and wrong in the conduct of persons and institutions. A business should be concerned with right and wrong performance in its conduct of affairs. An adequate code of ethics or concept of truth and morality, written or implied, becomes vital sooner or later to the ongoing of a business institution. Given the volume of business transacted, the producing and marketing of goods and services are conducted on a generally favorable level in the United States and Canada. There is little "under the table pay-off" in these countries, and there is appropriate attention given to guarantees about quality.

Our belief in ethical ideals is mingled with an understanding that there is a good deal of unethical conduct in business activity. Collusion, industrial espionage, patent infringement, price fixing, unapproved or inferior manufactures, and a score of other irregular or illegal practices do take place. Stealing in business is easier in the computer age. Ideas are easier to steal than things and computer chips are easier to steal than cattle. The public might easily believe, noting the stories appearing in the news media, that dishonesty is the common policy. Much of the unethical activity is the responsibility of one or a few individuals who, for greed, sacrifice their company and others. A manager or owner may follow unethical practices, but these commonly catch up with him in due course. Ultimately, he loses his business or his job and relinquishes the respect of the public he purports to serve.

The simplest human concept of ethics for business is based on customer expectations. A buyer has a fairly clear idea about what he wants in a product, and the manufacturer, if he is knowledgeable, is aware of purchaser expectations. Quoted at the opening of this chapter, the Golden Rule holds that as one would have his expectations met he should, when his own duty pertains, meet the expectations of others. Although the Golden Rule is a simple concept of ethics, it provides an important beginning for anyone. It is a basic summary, and from it inferences can be

drawn about means, treatment of laborers, efficient use of
public resources, and the like. That rule should characterize an ethical business, as it relates to the quality of the
product or service to be provided. Corporations, like "The
Golden Rule" in St. Paul, Minnesota, have sometimes
publicly used it as their guiding motto.

Corporate Ethics

A business should be scrupulously run. Honesty ought to
be basic policy. And there are ways of keeping that policy.
A business generally summarizes warranties for its products. It makes other statements on ingredients and
materials. It is a matter of ethics to fulfill those affirmations. The company ought to do what it promises to do.

When the ideals of management are not carried out by
the workers, the ethics of the company as a whole are commonly called into question. Perhaps a major problem in our
lifetime is that the public is conditioned to expect ideal
conduct from a business agency, but not from an individual. Since the rise of the corporation, the public has
tended to forgive individuals and blame institutions. When
ethics have been disregarded, the company is blamed. In
matter of fact, a company has no ethics except those of the
persons who administer it and work in it. Reinhold
Niebuhr touched on the contradiction when he stated that
we have a high opinion of human nature and low opinion
of human virtue. The public often adjusts the contradiction by crediting the good in man to his nature and the
lack of virtue to his institutions.

Tension rises when a company advertises its quality at a
high level and personnel produce at a low level. Workers
commonly take refuge behind the banner of the company.
Their conduct is somehow self-excused in the anonymity
of the corporation, and they release themselves from personal responsibility. The public omits these contradictions
in analyzing the company's business practices. The
conduct of individuals is blamed on the corporation.

This problem was dramatically illustrated to me during

World War II. I was employed during the summer between college years at the Firestone Tire and Rubber Company in Akron, Ohio. I worked along with several score others to clean neoprene gas tanks to be shipped to plants of the Curtis Wright corporation, where the tanks were installed in fighter planes. The tanks were self-sealing so that bullets passing through them would not cause either leakage or fire. Our job was to remove all plaster and paper that remained from the model or "jig" over which the tank was "built." From time to time a worker was somewhat careless (bored, or lazy, or both) and did not complete his assignment. The inspector (bored, or lazy, or both) missed his duty. The outgoing tank was a "time bomb." If sloshing gasoline loosened debris and that debris clogged the fuel line, the result would be the same as if an enemy had shot down an airplane of the United States. When the event did occur, all of the workers on the line were solemnized by the report. No one meant for the tragedy to happen, but it did. (The loss was never documented to us, but we accepted the report at the time.) If true, one or more of us on the line were responsible. The Firestone Company (whatever that is) did not want such a thing to happen. Only when the individual worker decided he would not fail in his assignment did we end the reports of "self-clogged lines." But some irresponsible workers excused themselves by stating it was Firestone's obligation. Firestone did hire tougher inspectors. And workers were held to more severe standards after the report.

Family Ethics

Basic ethics for the family are corporate ethics. The questions are: what is right and wrong for the group, and what is right and wrong for the individual in his group responsibility? The public sometimes perceives the guilt of a member as family corporate guilt, and vice versa. If a son violates personal or family standards, the family may suffer. And judgments are often made about the family from the conduct of its truant. What one does reflects good or ill on those closest to him. At least partial imputation is inevitable no matter how unfair. Today the individual may be unwilling to accept, and may be unaware of, his corporate duty to his family, just as workers may disregard or reject duty to employers—or employers to workers. In all these cases there appears general disregard for ethical duty. As it is in the modern corporation, unethical conduct is easier for the urban family than it was for the rural.

It is a matter of ethics, as well as wisdom, to give up personally whatever is within reason to gain benefits for the family. Members of a family are ethically bound to give up some of their time, some of their privacy, some of their labor, some of their money, some of their identity, so that they may receive some name, some comfort, some security, some service, some love from other members of the family. A family exists when there is a balance of privileges and duties between the one member and the many members. Without this dynamic exchange, persons may be related to each other, but they do not comprise a true family.

Even though unsatisfactory conduct in a child is sometimes taken as an administrative failure of a parent, principally the father, the Scriptures also point to a larger ethical issue. If the sins of the fathers are visited on several future generations, then a corporate moral issue follows the family. That morality can be affected for change by the spiritual life of family members: parents especially can affect it. Influence for good or ill is in the nature of things. At this point in history, scientists are making extensive investigation into genetic conditioning to discover if propensity for some kinds of human conduct, good or ill, may be introduced into the hereditary chain. If it can, there will be biological as well as social and biblical evidence for corporate morality in families. Depravity in society may be even more far-reaching than we believed it to be.

The parent is responsible, in this corporate sense, for the

actions of his child, at least to the degree that the parent is authorized to function. Until the child is an adult and on his own responsibility, there is a large ethic of duty that belongs to his family. How this is administered, the Apostle Paul believed, relates first to the spiritual life and ability of the husband/father. Failure does not mean personal moral failure, but corporate family failure. It is a failure of administration in the home and might portend failure for spiritual leadership in the church.

Stewardship Concepts

Ethics relates to the proper use of time and resources. The right use, the best use, of time and resources is presumed to be a higher or better ethical activity than lesser use. Some other use might not be unethical so much as less ethical in time. To use a resource to help persons in deep need is more highly ethical in time than helping those in lesser need, which is more ethical in priority than helping persons with no genuine need at all. Having awareness of these different levels of ethics improves decision making. For example, I may have to decide between two demanding options: to complete a professional assignment or to counsel one of my children. I find the decision as to what to do easier to make when I see the ethical duty before me. Further, there is often the matter of decision between two acceptable conclusions, a more difficult ethical exercise than deciding between overt or obvious good and evil.

For example, it is not possible not to pollute. The problem, we assume, relates to the amount of pollution. To keep pollution at the lowest possible level means operating on the highest ethical standard. The degree of excess in any human activity above or below the most efficient level is the degree of loss in ethics, if each person is responsible for his actions. Essentially, a responsible person is one who knows what he is doing and deports himself well for the benefit of others.

In a family one reaches for balance between alternatives. The wise man who can discover the balance between "not too much" and "not too little" succeeds as the ethical man making the best use of resources. He works enough, but not too much. He disciplines his children enough, but not too much, that they be not discouraged.

Moderation is a key principle. Each thing desired in my life relates to my virtue only when it is right and the result of measured investment. All my actions taken without some deliberation, even if their conclusions are pleasant, are accidental. There are many things a person might want, but if he is wise he is unwilling to give up more than so much time, so much freedom, so much money to get them. When the investment appears too great for the amount of return, the individual and the family will not pay the price. They should not. There is no "profit" in it.

There is an important factor in family corporate ethics that must be addressed, especially during historical periods when social welfare is large and easily available. When families are competent to care for their own members, they ought to do so. They do not shift the re-sponsibility to someone or anything else, even to an im-personal government. Not to carry my duty is, in some way, to dilute my character. I avoid, in such an instance, the opportunity to serve and shift it to another person or insti-tution.

Arguments for turning to the state are attractive to many people. We paid taxes so now we are drawing on our de-posits. Or, to pay our own way in emergency may eat up our resources. Or we do not wish to be dependent upon our family members. Or we have encouragement from those around us, even government, to utilize available programs. Any of these reasons may be available and legitimate. On occasion some are totally compelling. But they may be rationalizations to avoid duty, or they may be invoked to cover management failure. We remember that the Chrysler Corporation called upon government to save it, at a cost of hundreds of millions of dollars. Even though the govern-ment did rescue the company, at least for a time, the neces-sity implied poor or bungled management by Chrysler.

An illustration of excellence in management is provided
by Nehemiah. His goal was dramatic and monumental. His
resources were limited, and some were provided by the
government. His companions were volunteers, and the
problems as well as enemies were numerous. As his plan
progressed, he counted it both an achievement and a blessing from God that he could continue his work and accomplish his vision without help from the king.

In Nehemiah's experience there is something for all persons of faith. How may we best demonstrate our faith, and
the loving concern of God? We do so by working from the
smallest unit to the largest, not the reverse. What I can do
for myself, I will do ethically, so as to avoid hurting
others. What I cannot do for myself will be done by my
family members, unless they are unable or incompetent to
function. From that point we may turn to the larger community as the church or the local government. The last
resort is to large institutions like a federal government
managed from a distant center.

In some ways our preoccupation with largeness takes
away our sense of responsibility to manage our lives. We
can be anonymous in huge populations in government, in
schools, even in churches. The family is both small enough
and large enough to reveal me as one who lives, as one
who loves, as one who labors as God would have me to
live, love and labor.

That Sense of Balance

What may be done to motivate the family to become all
that it was meant to become? Answers to that question
have been addressed by way of business analogy in this
book. A corporation in business is like a corporation in the
family. A corporation learns to balance necessary alternatives, sometimes inevitable contradictions. A family is
drawn together as a whole unit—related individuals in a
caring group. Something of the individual is given up for
the group: something of the group is given up for him.
Individual rights are present, but are balanced with group

rights. To learn this balance is to learn how to live in most of our interpersonal relationships. It means learning citizenship.

The blessed sense of balance is a factor in maturity. In matter of fact, it is in the nature of all things. Seasons balance the earth in heat and cold, in sunshine and darkness, in wet and dry. A business balances between work and rest, producing and stopping production. Work for money (receiving) is balanced by work for others (giving).

A family must make choices as it considers worthwhile alternatives. As it chooses different options in different circumstances, it must arrive at a compromise of the right sort. At times the group choice goes against an individual's preference. At other times the group yields. Mature men and women know the legitimacy of the needs of self and others. They experience laughter and tears, health and pain, solemnity and mirth. They work out a balance of factors—expectations, learning, worshiping, and timing, among others—for family activities.

All is well when I have learned to manage myself. In managing myself well, in the context of my family, the family is also managed well. In managing my family well, I assist it to become a model, a model of Christ and His Bride, the Church. And that is good.

Reading about Ethics and the Family

Authors with Christian or generally Christian emphases:

Johnson, James. *The Nine to Five Complex*. Grand Rapids:
Zondervan, 1972.
Lee, Mark W. *Creative Christian Marriage*. Glendale,
Calif.: Regal, 1977. ("Faith that Fights Marriage,"
pp. 51-63; "Faith that Frees Marriage," pp. 65-80.)
_____. *How to Have a Good Marriage*. Chappaqua, N.Y.:
Christian Herald, 1978. ("Do you share the same religious beliefs?" pp. 57-61; "Are there any skeletons in
your closet?" pp. 62-65; "How will you handle re-
verses?" pp. 121-23; "Where do you plan to go to
church?" pp. 186-88; "How will you treat religious
differences between you?" pp. 188-91; "Are you willing to let God change your partner?" pp. 191-93.)
LeTourneau, Richard. *Keeping Your Cool in a World of
Tension*. Grand Rapids: Zondervan, 1975.

Authors with secular or generally secular emphases:

Bolles, Richard Nelson. *What Color Is Your Parachute?*
Berkeley, Calif.: Ten Speed Press, 1972.
Peters, Thomas J. and Waterman, Jr., Robert H.,
In Search of Excellence. New York: Harper & Row,
1981.

Works Cited

Anderson, Christopher. 1977. *The Name Game*. New York: Simon & Schuster. *Denver Post*. 1982. "Americans in the U.N.: 'Amateurs',", Associated Press, 8 June.

Dickens, Charles. *David Copperfield*. Chap. 12.

Goleman, Daniel. 1977. "Oedipus in the Board Room." *Psychology Today*. December.

Holt, John. 1980. "Growing up Engaged." *Psychology Today*. July.

Howard, Jane. 1978. *Families*. New York: Simon & Schuster.

Lee, Mark W. 1982. *Who Am I and What Am I Doing Here?* Milford, Mich.: Mott Media, Chap. 1.

Pascale, Richard Tanner and Anthony G. Athos. 1981. *The Art of Japanese Management*. New York: Simon & Schuster.

Pritchett, Richard. 1978. "Neuroses That Come with Your Name," *San Francisco Chronicle*. 17 November.

Rosemond, John. 1981. *Parent Power: A Common-sense Approach to Raising Your Children in the Eighties*. Charlotte, North Carolina: East Woods Press.

San Francisco Chronicle. 1982. "Joyce Hall, Hallmark's Founder, Dies." 30 October.

ServiceMaster Industries, Inc. 1981. Annual Report.

Sheppard, R.A. 1979. "The Pursuit of Happiness," a review of *The Culture of Narcissism: American Life in an Age of Diminishing Expectations*, by Christopher Lasch. *Time*. 8 January.

Tozer, A.W. *Wingspread*. 1943. Harrisburg, Pennsylvania: Christian Publications, Inc.

Tweedie, Donald F. Jr. 1976. "A Model for Marital Therapy," *Make More of Your Marriage*. (Gary R. Collins, ed.) Waco, Tex." Word.

Whitehead, Evelyn Eaton and James D. 1981. *Marrying Well*. Garden City, N.Y.: Doubleday.